D1575364

THE 'R' WORD

PROVOCATIONS

THE 'R' WORD

RACISM

SERIES EDITOR:
YASMIN ALIBHAI-BROWN

Biteback Publishing

First published in Great Britain in 2015 by
Biteback Publishing Ltd
Westminster Tower
3 Albert Embankment
London SE1 7SP
Copyright © Kurt Barling 2015

Kurt Barling has asserted his right under the Copyright, Designs and
Patents Act 1988 to be identified as the author of this work.

All rights reserved. No part of this publication may be reproduced, stored
in a retrieval system or transmitted, in any form or by any means, without
the publisher's prior permission in writing.

This book is sold subject to the condition that it shall not, by way of trade
or otherwise, be lent, resold, hired out or otherwise circulated without the
publisher's prior consent in any form of binding or cover other than that
in which it is published and without a similar condition, including this
condition, being imposed on the subsequent purchaser.

Every reasonable effort has been made to trace copyright holders of
material reproduced in this book, but if any have been inadvertently
overlooked the publishers would be glad to hear from them.

ISBN 978-1-84954-942-4

10 9 8 7 6 5 4 3 2 1

A CIP catalogue record for this book is available from the British Library.

Set in Stempel Garamond

Printed and bound in Great Britain by
CPI Group (UK) Ltd, Croydon CR0 4YY

For Kim,
Naomi, Nathaniel and Joseph
Keeping Hope Alive

Contents

'*Nigger* mind, go *black* home, you'll be all *white* in the morning.'

– Playground chant from the 1970s

Introduction

IN THIS BOOK I examine the orthodoxies that have shadowed my life but which I believe need to be roundly challenged. Hard as it may be to question orthodoxies, there will be no progress without such confrontation.

We live in a new information age where news travels fast, old ideas are subjected to constant disruption and the power of ideas can have an immediate and deep impact.

As a Londoner with English, Irish, Nigerian and German roots, I judge I can speak with some authenticity about the impact of skin colour on life in Britain. These are issues I have wrestled with personally and professionally for over fifty years. The simple daily challenges of life, the denigration and sheer wickedness often faced by people of colour in the past must not cloud our judgement on how to transform the prospects of future generations. I care deeply about the country that will provide a life for my children and their children when I am gone.

We people of colour, our families and friends, need to unchain ourselves from the history of oppression, from obsolete notions and language, and most of all from deeply ingrained divisions of 'them and us', Black and White, racism and anti-racism.

So let's start with how it was in my early lifetime. The rather unpleasant playground chant displayed at the start of this chapter gives a flavour of the times in the 1970s. The battle for playground equality reflected the broader daily social torture endured by people of colour throughout Britain.

At school, it was a throwaway line that a minority of bigoted White kids used to provoke you into a test of physical and mental toughness. It escalated easily and in adulthood it could lead to all sorts of accusations of 'chips on shoulders' and 'ungrateful foreigner' slights.

It formed part of the powerful myth that played out in many different walks of life that the colour of your skin made you inferior, and being White was something you could dream about but would forever be out of your reach. Not being White was presented as a social stigma. Learning to stand my ground toughened me up, physically and mentally, but I find it hard to imagine this would be acceptable banter in a playground today. Indeed, the consequences would be serious.

The consciousness of difference and the antipathy it caused in my mind to 'race' certainly began long before I had to put up with these daily micro-aggressions that all people of colour endured in 1960s and '70s Britain. The micro-aggressions nurtured a suppressed rage. It was common for people to describe me as having a chip on my shoulder when I argued back after being called 'half-caste', 'blackie', 'sambo', 'coon', 'nigger', 'wog', 'rubber-lips', 'fuzzy-head' or some other verbal slight from a veritable lexicon of racial filth. I can remember the day I discovered my 'wogness', which came as a complete surprise and left me winded on the primary school playground. I had a whole bag of chips on both shoulders by the time I reached my late teens. Fortunately, university and success re-educated me to deal with all those chips; to overcome an abject fear of failure imposed on me by the expectations of so many others just because of the colour of my skin. Others of my generation were perhaps not so fortunate.

Before I was conscious of it, my mother lost friends and associates and had to confront the realities of 'race' in 1960s Britain. But in her private world her son was neither Black nor White because she loathed 'racial' classification. She still hates it. Mothers and their children are linked by blood, which makes a mockery of racial divisions.

It is a worldview I have always respected, but not one I necessarily shared when I was dealing with playground bullies and politics. My mother was of the 'sticks and stones will break my bones, but words will never hurt me' persuasion. As far as I was concerned, this was demeaning nonsense when National Front supporters were battering me, and others like me. I confess, whilst I was busy trying to survive senseless racism and blatant discrimination, it made it hard to empathise with my mother's instinct that flesh and blood should not be subdivided into 'race'. But I've come to understand that 'race' and racism can undoubtedly exist one without the other, and this short book is my contribution to that debate.

I grew up in north London at a time of significant demographic change. Migration into Britain from the old empire was steady and growing and it was unsettling the patterns of living that imperial Britain had become used to over several centuries. Let's call it the *decolonisation* complex.

My mother is Anglo-Irish, born into a working-class Islington family. She is a die-hard Londoner who gave birth to a young baby of mixed heritage in 1961. Nothing really could prepare her for the world her son would come into, which was less liberal, more overtly prejudiced and firm in its caustic judgement on grounds of 'race' and miscegenation – a far cry from the more open-minded society we live in today.

It's hard to recall when the colour of my skin became an issue I needed to wrestle with. As a child I puzzled over how a person's differences could be entirely captured by skin colour. I think I must have instinctively disliked the notion of race. Of course, it didn't help when I discovered I was a 'wog'. It seemed to me skin colour was an arbitrary and poor guide to understanding my friends as individuals, so I got pretty mad – eventually indignant – at how others could so easily pass judgement on me. As a teenager, I became incensed when I was called a 'half-caste'. Half of what? I would ask. Or being told I was a kind of mongrel. It was no better if others tried to soften the blows of hurt with the idea that being a hybrid proved my vigour and potency. It was all equally nonsensical as far as I was concerned.

It wasn't made much better when the language changed to 'mixed-race'. Mixing evoked for me visions of watering down on the one hand and racial purity on the other. Neither of which seemed to me to have the slightest credibility in a world that had suffered the homicidal madness unleashed by the mythology of racial purity in Hitler's Germany. Millions died because of this idiocy, so why should I put up with an enduring racist hypocrisy in my life? Where, I asked myself, did all these codes emerge from? And how did we become so deeply entrenched in the language of raciology?

I can recall one of the customers on my schoolboy paper-round asking me (after delivering their paper for several years), in all seriousness, if my hair broke off when it got to a certain length or if I had it cut like normal (White) people. Yes, it sounds absurd, but it is a micro-aggression fact and some people really did need some kind of re-education. I never laboured under the delusion that re-education was impossible.

As a BBC journalist for over twenty-five years, it has been my experience that cultural norms and prejudices are merely replicated and propagated by the traditional national purveyors of society's so-called values. I have always had a thing for alternative narratives in public discourse. I seized every opportunity I could to use these alternative narratives to challenge the representation of people of colour in our social narratives; from soldiers in the Great War to the victims of crime, from Nelson's sailors to Lloyd's of London directors.

A particular news story throws this into sharp relief. The story of Rachel Dolezal, a young woman in the United States who, despite being White, had adopted the identity of being Black, became an international story of modern conceptions of difference. Millions of words were expended to criticise her, explain her decision and even to support her. Once upon a time, the answer to her identity question would have been, at the risk of appearing glib, black and white for everyone; clearly that is not the case today. What is perhaps just as interesting is why it became such a big headline-generating story at all. Could it be that the subtext was 'why on earth in this world would a White person want to be Black?' It's highly unlikely that a person of colour claiming to be White would have grabbed any news coverage, let alone headlines.

Perhaps my earliest sense of this absurdity is reflected in one of my mother's recollections from late 1965. In my early world most people were White. At nursery, that clearly started to make a difference in the way others perceived me. One day on the way home, sitting in the child seat on the back of my mother's bicycle, I shouted out to a nursery chum I'd spotted. He ignored me even after several attempts, at which point my mother heard me mutter to myself: 'He doesn't like me because of the colour of my skin. I wish my name was John and my hair was blond.'

I have often asked myself how a child of three could possibly know about skin colour. It was certainly off limits for my mother, still is as a matter of fact, but somehow I certainly must have felt different. This was probably the first stirring of the 'us and them' divide, which humanity so often places at the heart of its social interactions. I have often rationalised it as a child's defence mechanism against the micro-aggressions that I would soon come to consider as a normal part of everyday life. They would sow the seeds that would flower progressively into self-doubt. From my early teens I would then spend a dozen or so years trying to dig over that cultivated garden of prejudice and plant fresh seeds of ambition and hope.

Throughout my school years I became quite adept at disguising the doubt. I came to comport myself with confidence and even brashness. I was often described as cocky, and sometimes arrogant, but underneath it all were a lot of questions about identity, belonging and deep nagging doubts about whether I could elevate myself beyond the mediocrity so many people (but by no means all) seemed to expect of me.

Who was I, where did I fit in, could I keep getting up

when I was knocked back? Even as I became more comfortable in my own skin, others sought to challenge my self-assurance as if I was bucking the rules of the game. For some it was an affront that I could be so confident. I will never forget those others who made it their business to ensure that my confidence and resilience were bolstered (family aside), such as my secondary school head teacher Peter Targett, who insisted and saw to it that I made an excellent Head Boy.

Ironically, being of mixed heritage often made the game all the more complicated because people expected you to take sides. But there is injustice, inequality and discrimination and on those subjects I can most certainly take sides. How do we find resolutions to these enduring problems and does the stubborn mythology of race help or hinder that endeavour?

In any case, this is an essay exploring the impact of race and racism on people's lives. My experience as a journalist has taught me that there are always stories to tell which can present a particular point of view without revealing the truth of the wider picture. It was just such a story, on what I felt was inaccurate reporting on the Broadwater Farm riots in 1985, that brought me into journalism in the first place.

As my career developed over the years, I recognised that there are legions of people who remain in denial on all sides of the so-called race divide, who cannot help us heal the traumas of the past if they continue to live in that past. The language of race and racism are the unholy descendants of a false science, agreed. But how do we emerge out of the oppressiveness of the language of the past? What do we need in order to become a country that recognises difference, but accepts that the diversity of talent is not colour-coded? How do we ensure we can see the wood despite the trees? Does skin colour really explain everything in life's experience? Do the headlines on racism continue to reflect the underlying story, or is it just good copy?

Could it be that a headline-obsessed culture in a 24-hour-media environment only serves the immiseration of the debate on race and racism, where easy cliché leads to an increasing disconnect, considering so many of us embrace the living experience of mixed marriages, parenthood and inclusivity.

The organisation of the book

First, a point on definitions. Where possible I use the term BAME (Black, Asian and Minority Ethnic) throughout to denote those who are non-White in the classifications we use in the UK for statistical purposes. If I slip into the term Black it is shorthand for BAME unless I need to make a specific point, where I will use the appropriate descriptor.

In Part I, I will explore the evolution of the conceptual debates surrounding race. It is necessary to have a grasp of these debates to understand the power they have on our modern consciousness and the language we deploy and I will argue we remain largely trapped in. It will become clear that the debates have progressed and become more dismissive of the concept itself. In fact, there are those who have argued that because race is no longer credible as a concept, or a useful means of helping us understand social relations, we must have evolved into a post-racial society. The election of President Obama, some argue, proved this point. So, I will explore this idea of race, how we arrived at it being such a powerful moniker of difference and what we should make of it in today's world.

In Part II, I want to look more closely at the idea of racism itself. This 'post-racial' constellation has fuelled arguments that racism can no longer exist in its crude, old-fashioned sense, so using it as a means of understanding inequities, lack of opportunity and downright discrimination in society is no longer relevant. This presupposes that race is as socially or culturally irrelevant as it is biologically extinct. It suggests that we, contrary to a mountain of evidence, live in a world where skin colour no longer defines who we are or where we sit in the social hierarchy. But crude prejudice is not the problem so much as acting on it to elicit social discrimination or hate crime; to what extent has regulation infringed on the foul behaviour of some individuals? Has racism mutated into a new taxonomy of discriminatory habits and practices prompted by, for example, Islamophobia?

In Part III, I want to look at how we might change the language and perceptions of people associated with skin colour. A key arena is that of the media. Until the digital revolution created new paths of access to dissemination, the gatekeepers like the national broadcasters controlled the way we saw each other. Another key set of players in changing the flow of this debate has to be educators. But history has shown us these potential liberators have often been replicators of cultural norms not subversive of them.

Professor Kurt Barling
London, 2015

Part I:
Race

'The question of why people love what is like themselves and hate what is different is rarely asked seriously enough.'

– Theodor Adorno

M Y PURPOSE IN Part I is to try to get under the skin of what we mean by 'race' in modern Britain. To do that I will need to dig deep into the long evolution of this most challenging of concepts. There is so much 'common sense' ascribed to the meaning of that singular word that we have in effect created a modern reality out of a historical myth.

Unfortunately, people still take sides. Presumption often trumps reason and there are those who wilfully misinterpret race because they are simply too lazy or ignorant to think about their own prejudices. In these circumstances it is very easy to be in denial. But this absent-mindedness cuts both ways. There are those who, even faced with the evidence, believe racism is a thing of the past, that inequality and discrimination based on skin colour no longer exists. Equally there are those who think that race is all-encompassing and that every slight has racist roots. There are those who believe – despite the evidence – that little or no progress has been made since the 1960s. In a curious symbiosis, anti-racists and racists have come to rely on each other to preserve a set of orthodoxies that impoverish us all.

Of course, ignorance, prejudice and discrimination are not unique issues for people of colour. Only a fool would suggest that. Other classes of people experience discrimination, iniquitous circumstance and setbacks. Travellers, women, people with disabilities, lesbian, gay and transgender individuals can all tell their own stories of humiliation and hurt. But for people of colour it has always been impossible to outwardly disguise their difference, and this makes it all the more challenging to deal with people's perceptions because codes of race have made it possible for bigots to make a judgement before you've even had a chance to open your mouth. And because structural discrimination persisted for so long, the mental barriers that accompanied it have been peculiarly stubborn in coming down.

I'll use an unusual example to make my point about these psychological hangovers. Once as a junior producer working for the BBC, something that was still extraordinarily difficult in the 1980s and 1990s for a person of colour, I was charged with organising a debate on the disintegration of the former Yugoslavia. As a former LSE lecturer in International Relations, it was a subject on which I had some expertise. One of the issues it raised was the protection of minorities in the Balkans, and it seemed like a good idea to invite Enoch Powell (1912–98) on to the BBC panel.

The programme was broadcast as *New Nations, Old Hatreds* and it captured the spirit of both optimism and pessimism in the years following the fall of the Berlin Wall in 1989. But that is not the point of this story. As the person in charge of securing the guests and after a long telephone conversation and exchange of letters, I invited Enoch Powell to lunch at a very nice restaurant in Queen's Gate in Kensington. I arrived there before the anointed hour and when he arrived I approached him. I greeted him as the BBC producer and he asked if Dr Kurt Barling would be along soon. He was an unflappable politician, but he did do a double take when I said I was that very same person.

Enoch Powell, the politician most associated with introducing race into British politics (in reality 'race' was always at the heart of imperial policy), always insisted he was not a racist.

It was odd to find myself in the company of the anti-racists' devil incarnate. For the sake of accuracy I recall we had a very enjoyable lunch and a very robust exchange of views on the question of changing Britain in which I was not entirely gracious and Mr Powell, if uncomfortable, remained unflinching and extremely courteous.

In my conversation with him he said what he had always found improbable was that different groups could live alongside each other in a cultural bubble without that somehow exploding into conflict. In a historical sense, when we look at conflict around the globe Powell could point to more evidence that he was right than others could suggest he was wrong. In 1969, Powell was keen to distance himself from what he considered thuggish racism or even a xenophobic attitude. When asked whether he was a racialist, he clarified, 'If by a racialist you mean a man who despises a human being because he belongs to another race, or a man who believes that one race is inherently superior to another in civilisation or capability for civilisation, then the answer is emphatically no.'

Here I simply use the meeting as an example of Mr Powell's initial reaction, which was not untypical at the time. The surprise and looks on the faces of the other guests offered an insight into British racial expectations of the time. The juxtaposition of Mr Powell with a man of colour in a public place was seen as culturally counterintuitive.

I believe one of the drivers for change over the past decade has been the avalanche of diversity that has electrified the airwaves through ever-expanding digital platforms, in other words competition. This fresh and exciting content has shown vitality and embraced genuine difference in a way traditional providers were incapable of. Arguments about representation on the BBC and other networked broadcasters become a function of power and gatekeeping, not about a need to open up society to the glorious technicolor world we actually live in. That is being done by a revolution in social media. Representation is under assault from what I shall call in this book *'creative disruption'*. I've yet to read any really convincing research on the implications of the digital revolution on the perceptions of difference. They can't be long in coming, surely? The consequence of all this for broadcasters is that change is no longer an option but a means of survival. In this book I want to introduce what I think will be a key driver of change through this idea of 'creative disruption'.

Nevertheless, this 'creative' assault on normative assumptions is helped by the proliferation of media outlets, but in particular social media, where people of colour can see themselves reflected back in a multitude of ways broadcasters couldn't begin to achieve. So little research has been done on the impact of this 'disruption' that so far we can only speculate on the ways in which this will reshape the social discourse on 'race'. Here I will only be able to tease out the argument. There is certainly hope that it will start to make the categories of 'race' look as absurd as they are unscientific.

Dyed-in-the-wool racists say that it is not nurture

or the environment that determines these things, but nature. I once had a very serious, on-the-record BBC interview with Canadian professor J. Philippe Rushton, who had coincidently studied for his PhD at my alma mater,[1] in which he insisted that Blacks are not born as intelligent as Whites. Not a man to endear himself to me.

As this section charts the study of races known as 'raciology' and the conceptual history of 'race', we will discover that there has been nothing solid or permanent about the concept of 'race' since it first came into common usage in the English language, possibly with the translation of the early works of German philosopher Immanuel Kant (1724–1804).[2]

More importantly, we shall see it has constantly changed to reflect the culture within which it is utilised. It has meant different things in different places and at different times, although in Britain for the past half

---

1   London School of Economics & Political Science. More on this exchange later.

2   E. C. Eze, *Journal of the History of Ideas*, Vol. 61, No. 4, 2000.

century we have adopted many American codes, despite significant cultural variations, of which the history of slavery is the most significant one in this discourse on race.

By way of a simple example, the science in these matters has overwhelmingly concluded that colour of skin does not determine intelligence. Nevertheless, experience shows that people's belief in the intelligence argument has little to do with that science and more to do with the myths, old wives' tales and everyday humour which encompass difference.

Writing in 1897, W. E. B. Du Bois (1868–1963), the great African-American writer and philosopher, referred to 'racial' differences as the alternative appearances of 'color, hair and bone'. At its most simplistic level, racism implies or asserts an intrinsic connection between the way people look and what they think and can do, all the way from how well you dance, run, work, how 'civilised' you are, even how intelligent groups of people are, as defined by these observable 'racial' characteristics.

Part I cannot overlook the real impact of racism nor the reality that something in our social interactions has reinvented the idea of 'race' in the imagination of successive generations. Eminent cultural theorist and sociologist Stuart Hall captured this characteristic of race by calling it a 'floating signifier', an idea in permanent transition reflecting society's constantly mutating imagination around the word 'race'.[3]

The history of 'race'

But this is not to start the story at the beginning. The concept of 'race' didn't just happen – it evolved. For this we need to wind the clock back to the first encounters between different peoples – that is to say, between divergent cultures – which happened in the discovery of the New World by the Old.

Stranger fear (the actual meaning of xenophobia) is as old as the hills. We have always lived in tribes linked through kith and kin, and fear of the other has an entirely rational history in human societies as the basis

---

3   S. Hall, 'Race: The Floating Signifier', Lecture at Goldsmiths, University of London, 1997.

for reinforcing kinship and securing survival. When you combine this with the human quest since the Enlightenment to build knowledge around systems of scientific classification, you can begin to see the first rounds in the evolution of the concept of 'race'.

The Spanish 'conquistadors' were supported and financed by the state in Spain and the Catholic Church provided the moral framework for the earliest debates on the difference between the Spanish and the peoples they had encountered in the New World. In this world, Christianity lay at the heart of European conceptions of the known universe.

In the debates within the Catholic Church, Juan Ginés de Sepúlveda (1489–1573) asked, 'Are these true men?' He was posing the question in the biblical sense. Are these people in the New World the same species or some other manifestation of creation?[4]

It is in these accounts of the first meetings between Columbus and the aboriginal peoples of the Americas

---

4   It took around two centuries to recognise that these peoples might be
    exactly the same kind of human, when the abolitionists raised such questions
    under the conditions of slavery.

that historians often start their endeavours to understand debates surrounding the conceptions of difference.
The debates at this point mark a transition because the
Catholic Church was asked to intervene and determine
whether the inhabitants of the New World were part
of the same species.

Pitted against the views of Sepulveda, who saw these
peoples as non-rational and closer to the apes and therefore useful only as slaves, were those of Bartolomé de las
Casas (1484–1566). Las Casas reasoned that the 'natives'
were fully human and needed conversion and, although
not equals, were capable of reason, emotions and pain
in the same way as the Spanish.

The Las Casas view held sway and became an enduring modus vivendi for Western civilisation until the age
of reason, rationalism and science started to grapple
with these differences.

Until the Enlightenment, superstition and religion
continued to rule the moral consciousness of men and
in this sense a hierarchy of the colonisers over the colo-
nised people was given moral justification by invoking
the need to save the souls of these beings for the Church.

It of course suggests that even then men of conscience needed to justify their actions somehow – 'Ah, yes, they were men, but they were inferior.'

The Age of 'Enlightenment and Reason'

Take a stroll through the introductory galleries at the British Museum in London and you will see how exceptionally well they illustrate how the early scientists – who were mostly what we might now call polymaths – made classification the root of science and scientific methodology. Quantitative science needs to identify, deconstruct, count and measure in order to create a meaningful way of understanding what we observe in the natural world. The triumph of science was to construct a rigorous, testable method to do this – scientific method – to help us make sense of the natural world.

Until the natural sciences evolved as an academic discipline with the work of, amongst others, Sir Isaac Newton (1642–1727), the prevailing wisdom was that the world was 6,000 years old. We believed living creatures sprang from the elements and people were only just getting used to the idea that the sun and the universe didn't revolve around the Earth.

René Descartes (1596–1650), one of the instigators of the French Enlightenment and the father of the 'age of rationalism', deployed rational, defensible argument to challenge the centuries of superstition and religion of the pre-Enlightenment existence of humanity. Through the process of establishing classifications from the objective study of difference in the natural world – including humankind – scientists began to reorder the way society understood the world it inhabited. Without this classification, the world about us would now seem meaningless; it is what Stuart Hall described as an 'elemental cultural impulse', giving us a sense of the cultural function of science.

Scientists and philosophers were often one and the same person wrestling with attributing existential meaning to the differences that their scientific endeavours were busy evidencing in their exploration of the natural world. Looking at the texts of the time we can discern that 'race' from its inception was skewed because those early scientists and philosophers shared their new ideas within their narrow circles. So Kant would seek to build on the work of Hume, who would draw inspiration from the biological discoveries of Linnaeus (1707–78). If you will, the philosophers became the 'spin doctors' for the emerging natural sciences.

Despite the fact that their exposure to people of colour was in all likelihood negligible or non-existent, the likes of Immanuel Kant and David Hume (1711–76) waxed lyrically and ascribed judgements to skin colour in a generic rather than a particular sense. Hume in *Of National Characters* (1754) declared:

> I am apt to suspect the negroes in general and all species of men (for there are four or five different kinds) to be naturally inferior to the whites. There never was a civilised nation of any other complexion than white ... No indigenous manufactures among them, no arts, no sciences. On the other hand, the most rude and barbarous of the whites, such as the ancient Germans, the present Tartars, have still something eminent about them ... Such a uniform and constant difference could not happen ...

if nature had not made an original distinction between these breeds of men.[5]

Perhaps they were working on instinct, but it gives the lie to the notion that the Enlightenment was a system of virtuous thinking for all men. Or that great minds cannot be brought low by fundamental ignorance.

Science was of course a counterblast to the biblical interpretations explaining all creation, and in this changing public debate during the Enlightenment, as philosophers and scientists embraced and consolidated the idea that all human beings belonged to one species, a subversive and misdirected assumption was that it was of fundamental importance to mark the differences within the species. Science created the myth that it was somehow neutral. The science of race is a strong indicator that science is not and has never been culturally neutral.

---

5   Quoted in E. C. Eze, op. cit., pp. 691–8.

The birth of scientific raciology

In a dramatic break with the biblical understandings of the past, scientists approached humankind in much the same way as every other living being in the natural world. They created a taxonomy to organise what was different on the surface as later described by W. E. B. Du Bois without yet being able scientifically to get beneath the skin.

In 1735, Linnaeus had set out his scientific critique that there were divergences of talent between 'races', which he classified as: Homo Europaeus (Whites), who he said were lively and ruled by custom; Homo Americanus (Native Americans), who were tenacious, contented and governed by habit; Homo Asiaticus (Asians), who were stern, greedy and led by opinion; and Homo Afer (Africans), who were cunning, slow, careless and ruled by caprice.

The following excerpt from the 1792 English edition of his work established the connection between appearance and temperament:

Homo Europaei. Of fair complexion, sanguine

temperament and brawny form ... of gentle manners, acute
of judgement, of quick invention and governed by fixed
laws. Homo Afri. Of black complexion, phlegmatic temperament and relaxed fibre. Of crafty, indolent and careless
disposition and are governed in the actions by caprice.[6]

It is hard to imagine that the early scientific community would have radically challenged the existing imperial political dispensation and in these circumstances the categories were essentially a readymade explanation for the hierarchy that already existed rather than suggesting that that hierarchy might be wrong. This early work tried to establish the similarities between different groups of human beings and asked who was essentially closest to the ape. No prizes for guessing the hierarchy those early anthropologists came up with: Whites at the top and Blacks at the bottom.

So, science unsurprisingly validated European supremacy, which in crude racial terms meant 'White

---

6   Quoted in A. Rattansi, *Racism: A Very Short Introduction* (Oxford University Press, 2007), p. 26.

supremacy' and ambitions. Rather than challenging these assumptions through the discovery of fresh evidence as science developed as a field of enquiry, specialisms proliferated and tended to reinforce the established taxonomies. Science began to be used in the service of racial hierarchies that were becoming embedded in the imperial view of the world in Britain.

Paul Broca (1824–80) and Arthur de Gobineau (1816–82) were French anatomists very much considered to be the fathers of 'scientific racism'; the idea they first developed was that the races of mankind can be classified, and their value judged, on the basis of biological traits.

They built on the scientific enquiries of the father of evolutionary theory Charles Darwin (1809–82). Darwin was an inveterate explorer who gathered information from across the known world, which he collated into knowledge and his novel theory of evolution, otherwise known as Darwinism.

Gobineau mixed these ideas of Darwin with the Victorian notions of class in his *Essay on the Inequality of the Human Races*, concluding that:

The social order is founded upon three original classes, each of which represents a racial variety; the nobility, a more or less accurate reflection of the conquering race; the bourgeoisie, composed of mixed stock coming close to the chief race; and the common people who live in servitude or at least a very depressed position. These belong to a lower race which came about in the south through miscegenation with the Negroes and in the north with the Finns.[7]

Robert Knox (1791–1862), a prominent Edinburgh physician, became interested in ethnological, zoological and medical research whilst he was an army surgeon in Europe and South Africa. As an early proponent of 'race science', he published *The Races of Men* (1850), in which he argued that 'race was everything' and humanity was divided into separate races, whose ability to live in a civilised way was very different.[8] In Europe,

---

7   Quoted in S. Jones, *In the Blood: God, Genes and Destiny* (Flamingo, 1996), p. 172.

8   Knox was discredited not for his work in race science, but for his association with Burke and Hare, who were convicted of murdering the people whose bodies they made available to Knox for anatomical science dissections.

Knox developed fresh hierarchies between Scandinavians, Celts and Slavs.

Along with Gobineau and Broca's studies, a body of work emerged that insisted that humankind could be divided into a limited number of distinct and permanent races, and that race was the key concept for an understanding of human variation. These scientists focused on the visible physical markers that characterised the different races, especially skin colour, facial features, texture of hair and, with the growing influence of phrenology, the size and shape of the skull.

'Race' in the cultural firmament

By the nineteenth century it is clear that it was becoming difficult to disaggregate the relationship between science, culture and race. Scientific method, however clear it aimed to be, began to fundamentally distort what it was we were to understand from an abundant human cultural diversity that scientists accepted existed.

Cliché and prejudice quickly entered the language

of 'race'. Edmund Burke (1729–97) talked of 'the very different civility of Europe and China. The barbarism of Tartary and of Arabia and the savage state of North America and New Zealand.'

Already in the late 1700s, Immanuel Kant, a great admirer of his contemporary Scottish philosopher David Hume, continued to propagate ideas that were rooted in both men's instincts rather than science. The mixing of races was presented as folly and suicidal for civilisation:

> The Negroes of Africa have by nature no feeling that rises above the trifling. Mr Hume challenges anyone to cite a single example in which a Negro has shown talents, and assert that among the hundreds of thousands of blacks who are transported elsewhere from their countries, although many have been set free, still not one was ever found who presented anything great in art or science or any other praiseworthy quality, even though among the whites some continually rise aloft from the lowest rabble, and through superior gifts earn respect in the world. So fundamental is the difference between

these two races of man, and it appears to be as great in regard to mental capacities as in colour.[9]

This is how science and philosophy, prejudice and myth, blended the physical and the philosophical into a powerful argument and the emerging study of races – raciology   which required enlightenment and myth to be intertwined.

Early raciologists believed they needed to deal with the question of whether the variations they noted within races were as significant as the differences that might exist between them. And how might man deal with these differences socially? Kant, for example, gave stark warnings against miscegenation. He invoked a natural law argument that the races should be kept apart:

This we can judge with probability that the intermixture of races (caused by large-scale conquests), which gradually extinguishes their characteristics, does not seem

---

9   From I. Kant, *Observations on the Feeling of the Beautiful and Sublime*, quoted by S. Jones, op. cit.

beneficial to the human race – all pretended philan-
thropy notwithstanding. Instead of assimilation, which
was intended by the melting together of various races,
Nature has here made a law of just the opposite. In the
nation of the same race, instead of allowing the characters to develop constantly and progressively toward
resembling one another, whereby ultimately only one and
the same portrait would result as in prints taken from the
same copperplate, Nature has preferred to diversify infi-
nitely the characters of the same stock.[10]

So commonplace were these characterizations and
emerging beliefs that inheritors of the philosophical
mantel of Kant, Hume and Georg Hegel (1770–1831),
such as Karl Marx (1818–83), also assumed the correctness of the embedded relationships of difference and
inferiority based on 'racial' differences. These values
and prejudices were, for example, reflected in a letter
to his collaborator Friedrich Engels (1820–95). Marx

---

10 Quoted in P. Gilroy, *Between Camps: Nations, Cultures and the Allure of Race* (Penguin, 2000).

complains about 'the Jewish nigger' philosopher Ferdinand Lassalle (1825–64):

> It is now quite plain to me – as the shape of his head and the way his hair grows also testify – that he is descended from the negroes who accompanied Moses's flight from Egypt (unless his mother or paternal grandfather interbred with a nigger … Now this blend of Jewishness and Germannesss, on the other hand, and basic negroid stock, on the other, must inevitably give rise to a peculiar product. The fellow's importunity is also niggerlike.[11]

These philosophers were trying to create meaning in the human world from the taxonomy and biological classification that had been created by the father of modern biology Carl Linnaeus.

More importantly, they associated each race with innate and distinct cultural, social and moral traits.

---

11 Letter from Karl Marx to Friedrich Engels, quoted in F. Wheen, *Karl Marx* (Fourth Estate, 1999), p. 248. It is rather disconcerting to realise that competence in one discipline does not, even with great thinkers, mean competence in all fields of intellectual endeavour.

Perhaps influenced by the ideas in political philosophy espoused by his contemporary Marx, Gobineau conflated race and class to suggest that the social order was created by competition and struggle between races. The result was inevitably the conquest of one race over all others.

It is certainly worth noting that at the same time, these scientists were also developing theories of the inferiority of women based on skull and brain size, low brain weight and deficient brain structures associated with those of 'lower races' as a means of explaining the prejudice that women possessed inferior intellectual abilities.

A kind of false consciousness evolved in what by modern standards was pretty crude scientific method. The conclusions drawn from this 'scientific' approach became embedded in our cultural understanding of difference and human diversity and these played out as prejudices within cultures on the basis that the science described a reality, which it most certainly did not.

'Race' and the global political economy

The late 1800s was a time when European empires and

conquest were often brutally militarily imposed, with poor regard for the lives of those who were defeated or dared to resist. Whilst the British imperial design began with trade, its political imperatives necessitated maintaining clear differentiation between the rulers and the ruled.

As William Dalrymple observed, in the early days of the Indian Raj, some of the 'White Mughals' happily married local women and adapted to rather grand princely lifestyles, as well as providing for their mixed-heritage offspring.[12] But, whilst in the early parts of the imperialist project it was not uncommon for British men to take Indian women as wives or concubines when the East India Company was concerned about profit, it was increasingly frowned upon as the politics of supremacy dovetailed with ideas of 'race'. By the time the colonisation of Africa was in full progress, there was a distinct hierarchy, with White British at the top and Black Africans at the bottom. Different parts of

---

12 W. Dalrymple, *White Mughals: Love and Betrayal in Eighteenth-Century India* (HarperCollins, 2002).

the empire – particularly in the Caribbean and Africa – invented their own conventions on the racial gradations in between.

Let us not forget, the Americas are seen as the continents of slavery, but it was the British Empire (along with the French, Spanish and Portuguese) that established the trade in North America and the Caribbean. It was English laws and Parliament that governed the Americas and the Caribbean for much of the early history of North America. Even the founding fathers of the United States were born British.

Successful imperial expansion gave a kind of legitimacy to the idea that there was a racial superiority and the language of empire and trade would reinforce this prejudice in its expansion of cultural message in its advertising for items such as soap. One such advert depicted the bleached whiteness of an African's skin after the application of soap. As if cleansed black skin would turn white.

The imagery of such advertisements would have reinforced the popular mythology of Black inferiority and White superiority. This established a pattern of 'race-thinking'[13] that in turn underpinned patterns of discrimination, racism and unconscious bias in Britain and all its Dominions and more broadly in a Eurocentric view of humanity.

'Race' was increasingly used to justify White supremacy and to explain that some groups were 'superior' to other 'inferior' groups. Biological difference was a way to justify this hierarchy of races, which unsurprisingly matched the colonial dispensation.

Between the 1880s and 1930s, the burgeoning imperial projects gave a social and political context for the movement in Europe and the USA that dubbed itself Social Darwinism, which evolved into the Eugenics movement. Rather than probing the science inherited from Linnaeus, Francis Galton (1822–1911) – a cousin of Charles Darwin – accepted the parameters of this racial science and tried to develop and finesse it.

Eugenicists began to draw on the ideas of animal husbandry, believing that selective breeding of human beings might ensure that the so-called pure bloodlines

13   Part III expounds on the idea of 'race-thinking' after the ideas of Jacques Barzun.

of Englishmen, Frenchmen, or White Northern Europeans in the case of America, could be maintained in an era when empire was making the mixing of peoples ever more probable. It was an existential argument that conflated culture and biology to a political end.

Progressively the USA and parts of the British Empire such as Canada and Australia dominated by White migrants introduced restrictions into their immigration policies to try to ensure that the type of people allowed in would not contaminate the 'Whites only' philosophy to preserve their 'racial' integrity and their 'good blood'.

By now 'race' was firmly part of accepted wisdom but it was about to face its toughest test after centuries of consolidation. It wasn't such a big step from this type of eugenics thinking to the 'racial hygiene movement' in Germany, which developed its anti-Semitic doctrine using much of the work of eugenicists. Although the Nazis sought to discriminate and dehumanise the Jews, who were a well-established part of European civilisation, they often justified the exclusion of Jews from all walks of life in Germany by referring to the way Blacks in the United States and colonials in the empires of other European nations were excluded.

The essence of the Nazi philosophy on 'racial hygiene' as laid out by Alfred Rosenberg (1893–1946)[14] was that the purity of the German race was sacrosanct and that this logically meant the state had to rethink public policy in order to conform with these imperatives. Professors of biology, medicine, history, political science and philosophy all staffed the various Nazi institutions that worked through the Nuremberg Laws passed in 1935 to systematically discriminate against and dehumanise Jews and prevent contamination of a 'pure bloodline'.

It may have required the suspension of critical thinking by many, but such was the power of the idea of 'racial hygiene'. Indeed, so wedded were rational scientists to the concept of 'racial purity' that very quickly sterilisation was recommended for perceived forms of 'physical degeneracy' and, ultimately, the 'final solution' to stop

---

14 Alfred Rosenberg was a philosopher and chief ideologue of the Nazi Party. He was hanged at Nuremberg for crimes against humanity, in particular his role in the 'Final Solution' of the Jewish question.

the contamination of the 'pure' Aryan race by the total extermination of the Jews.[15]

The Holocaust brought the political credibility of eugenics and scientific racism to a crashing halt. Both were rightly blamed for the Nazi excesses. But despite the widespread abhorrence of what the Nazis had done, there was still widespread academic support and a popular understanding that there was a scientific foundation for the division of humankind into separate races with different, stable, biologically inherited characteristics.

Deference towards science, scientists and scientific method had framed the debates on 'race', but the devastating consequences led for the first time to an international attempt to confront the specious studies of raciology. It was recognised that the problem of 'race-thinking' had become embedded in cultural outlooks. Science might have legitimated such 'race-thinking', but

15 It's worth noting that Nazi propaganda often made the claim they were doing nothing more than America and European imperial powers did with their Blacks. A political defence for scientific nonsense, but this was not a political crime unique to Germany and the Germans.

it was confused and unsystematic, although presented as rational, coherent and authoritative.

The United Nations, through the offices of UNESCO (United Nations Educational, Scientific and Cultural Organization), challenged the credibility of scientific racism and after much deliberation in 1950 recommended that humanity should reject the scientific validity of racial classification as the basis of understanding human differences. The doctrine it drafted emphatically asserted the equality of men and races and a programme of 'disseminating scientific facts, designed to remove what is generally known as racial prejudice'.[16]

So science, philosophy and history, along with social and economic transformation in Europe and America, juxtaposed with the Western world's domination of non-Europeans, shaped a world view at the turn of the twentieth century that framed the language of relations between the 'races' in which we remain to a large degree 'imprisoned'.

---

16 The UNESCO doctrine was heavily influenced by exiled German-Jewish scholars like anthropologist Franz Boas, who believed culture rather than genetics underpinned human variation. Cited by J. Entine, *Abraham's Children: Race, Identity and the DNA of the Chosen People* (Grand Central, 2008).

How the American experience has skewed the 'race' debate

The question of exactly how much the institution of slavery contributed to the way in which 'race' as an ideology evolved is widely disputed. Slavery and colonial domination were nevertheless fundamental features of the developing global political economy in the 1700s and 1800s.

It is clear that the supporters of the slave trade legitimised it as an institution by drawing on popular scientific notions that Africans were inferior. The development of the slave economies of the Caribbean and America simply reinforced these views over several centuries. The popular refrain across European empires became that it had become their duty to help civilise the world they were colonising.

The collective endeavours of scientists, philosophers and politicians to embed racial classifications in our culture arguably ended up justifying the use of racist power through the institution of slavery. Scientists such as Linnaeus would have needed to challenge several centuries of practice and a global economy predicated on a slave system and European colonial expansion to come up with a theory of racial differentiation that differed from a highly organised system of hierarchical social relations with Europeans on top and everyone else below.

The history of human societies has been that hierarchical classification has always been a way of maintaining a social order. It harboured a rational preservation strategy, where communities that organised themselves into groups could defend themselves against outsiders. The aristocracy ruled with the help of the barons, who lorded it in turn over the feudal serfs in much of Europe's medieval tribal existence.

In the age of Enlightenment, as Britain and other European powers sought to build global empires, these classifications may have become more complex and global, but were still used in the time-honoured way to exercise the use of power. So the colonial classification of human beings along racial lines fitted into the traditional deployment of power.

It is incontrovertible that as a consequence of the institution of slavery, large fortunes were amassed by slave traders and planters, which in turn played a significant part in ensuring that Britain became the pre-eminent industrial economy, banking centre and dominant political and military power in the world. Most Britons find it hard to accept the idea that these privileges embedded structures of wealth and behaviour which left a legacy of inequality, discrimination and racism.

Blood, Blackness and colour codes

In those societies where slavery formed the basis of the differentiation between European and African heritage, any amount of African ancestry or blood meant an individual found himself or herself classified as Black (USA, Brazil, Caribbean).

It became known as the 'one drop' of blood rule that suggested any amount of African heritage classified an individual as Black and came to consolidate the classifications between Black and White. In Hispanic communities it was common to talk about *mulattos*, a synonym for hybrid. And there was a detailed nomenclature for shades of all descriptions in between so-called 'pure' European and 'pure' African. 'One drop' is a notion that endures to this day.

This system of classification quickly helped to entrench widespread prejudice and discrimination. To fight this racism has taken a century of activism. To fight against White supremacy, people – predominantly Black people – had to organise themselves to try to challenge the consequences of the classification.

By the time America had fought its Civil War and slavery had been abolished, it was clear that there would be no mixing of Whites and Blacks, and law and convention was used to ensure that the differentiation underpinned by slavery persisted after emancipation. In the later part of the nineteenth century and the early part of the twentieth, this agenda became even more confused with an elongated 'racial' hierarchy that also classified those with Irish and Italian heritage as Black. 'Blackness' was socially constructed to reinforce conventions of differentiation, but acted only as a proxy rather than a synonym for 'race'.

In the field of political struggle, the *sina qua non* of defending the rights of Black people was the assumption that all non-White people had common ground in the fight against White supremacy. In this sense it became a dialectical struggle between opposites – the racist versus the anti-racist struggle.

Whilst anti-racist activists necessarily used the categories of the oppressor to liberate the oppressed, Black political struggle is not about biology but about justice and equality. Black in this sense refers to a long history of political oppression and not genetic determinism. Nowhere has this been more sharply defined than in the civil rights struggles in the United States. As a consequence, the evolution of an American 'racial discourse' has informed much of the race debate in late twentieth-century Western civilisation.

This now presents us with an existential problem. Biology has made a nonsense of race. It begs the question of whether political activism should reassess what it is that is being fought for rather than against. As the race classification has become increasingly suspect, the political struggle that arose out of that dialectical struggle suggests that Black rights is a struggle of ever-decreasing circles, as race becomes a less effective 'signifier' to

mobilise people. Instead, we see an increasing adherence
to the politics of identity, a fundamental Achilles heel
of the multiculturalism that emerged in 1970s Britain.

Historical understanding matters because it is this
long history that makes the debates on race and science so deeply ingrained. It is why we talk of 'common
sense' even though it is nothing of the sort. These are
accepted wisdoms that have been passed down through
several centuries of practice, such as views on marriage
or homosexuality. They are difficult to shift.

We face a modern choice on how we approach 'race',
given the changes that we have seen in our understanding
over the past fifty years since the UNESCO declaration. We need to accept the verdict of the biological
sciences – where 'race' was initially central to differentiating humankind – which have rejected the proposition
that physiological differences do provide a rational and
scientific basis for classifying human races into separate subcategories.

Either we accept that difference is so endemic in the
world around us there is little point in denying it as a
point of meaningful differentiation, or 'race' is really

only a reality in the context of the way we identify differences and use our language, which bear little resemblance to the widely accepted scientific view of human diversity.

This is at the heart of Stuart Hall's conception of race as a cultural signifier, as he argues:

> Race works like a language and signifiers refer to the system and concepts of the classification of a culture to its [meaning-making] practices. And those things gain their meaning, not because of what they contain in their essence, but in the shifting relations of difference, which they establish with other concepts and ideas in a signifying field. Their meaning because it is relational and not essential can never be finally fixed, but is subject to the constant process of redefinition and appropriation.[17]

That leaves us with the legacy of old language and inherited systems of meaning in popular discourse. At most this bequeaths a fluid discursive concept where

17 S. Hall, op. cit.

differences and their acquired meanings remain a factor in human culture and may regulate our conduct. But we need to challenge this persistent ideology if we want to reshape our social relations.

It follows if we challenge and reconfigure our knowledge of difference, it will transform meaning and understanding so that 'race' per se will stop being seen as something that should shape the behaviours and interactions between peoples and cultures in a pluralistic society such as Britain.

'Race' – a stubborn survivor

Race is a social construction. It has proven remarkably resistant to rationality, activism and common sense. In popular discussion it is often used to identify personal or national characteristics. Off-the-cuff racial distinctions are seen as real and indisputable. In health matters and sport – and in some circles intelligence – particular characteristics are still being associated with what we commonly call 'races'.

So, for example, there are particular diseases, such as

sickle-cell anaemia, which afflicts African and Caribbean population groups, or even Tay-Sachs syndrome, which has been found to be prevalent within particular Jewish communities.[18] Some population groups do have distinct commonalities but these are not sufficiently widespread or linked to particular physiological commonalities to be regarded as racial groupings in the typical sense of that category. They are neither indicative or definitive.

In sport, too, the success of Caribbean and African-American sprinters on the one hand, such as Usain Bolt, and Kenyan long-distance runners on the other has raised questions about Black superiority in sporting endeavour. Although it can be argued that distinct and delineated population groups might have specific physiological advantages or genetic dispositions, this doesn't provide evidence of the powerful and potent notion of racial difference.

There are virtually no Kenyan 100m or 200m sprinters or Caribbean 10,000m or marathon stars for this very

---

18 J. Entine, op. cit.

reason. Even here the evidence undertaken by sports physiologists is inconclusive. It is population group-defined, not racial and Black. There are as likely to be genetic similarities between Jamaicans and Welshmen as Kenyans and Nigerians. Others such as Ellis Cashmore[19] argue that it is the will to win in competitive societies and the opportunities presented to young athletes that will determine success rather than 'race'.

But it is partly because of these popular debates that not all modern scientists have abandoned the idea that science can explain the differences between social groups or races. It is worth noting they tend not to be biologists.

So whilst the world's leading geneticists such as Steve Jones at University College London have argued that there is no biological, physiological or genetic definition of race that is sustainable scientifically speaking, there are those who have continued to argue that there is a genetic explanation for social, cultural or even personal behaviour.

---

19   E. Cashmore, *Making Sense of Sports* (Routledge, 2000).

When I interviewed J. Philippe Rushton for a BBC film we called *The Faster Race*[20] (the title was ironic), he made claims based on his research as a psychologist that by measuring brain size and genitalia you could identify racial differentiations which explained why Blacks were less intelligent, less sexually restrained and less law-abiding that Asians and Whites.[21]

In 1994, *The Bell Curve*, written by Richard Herrnstein and Charles Murray, made the startling claim that the legions of the American poor are to blame for their own predicament because they are hindered by their genetic or biological inheritance. Herrnstein and Murray tried to avoid the issue of race directly by focusing on poverty. Whilst poverty and skin colour do not always coincide, it is often a code word for Black:[22]

---

20 K. Barling, *The Faster Race*, BBC2, September 2000; J. P. Rushton, *Race, Evolution and Behavior: A Life History Perspective* (Transaction Books, 1995).

21 It must have been an interesting experience for him being interviewed by a four-man television crew all with African heritage. I confess this was one of the only interviews I conducted for the BBC where I nearly lost my temper. Rushton died in 2012.

22 This is despite the evidence that there are more middle-class affluent African-Americans than those who live in poverty.

> The technically precise description of America's fertility policy is that it subsidises births among poor women, who are also disproportionately at the low end of the intelligence distribution. We urge generally that these policies, represented by the extensive network of cash and services for low-income women who have babies, be ended. The government should stop subsidising births to anyone rich or poor.[23]

Although *The Bell Curve* reignited the debate about race and intelligence, in reality it did very little to resolve it. Herrnstein and Murray argued the evidence showed that across Black and White America there were widely varying IQ scores. They reached a conclusion that said that Blacks were significantly behind Whites. But their methodology, although creating controversy, could not deal with the simple question – why?

In particular, they failed to reflect on those parts of the African-American population where scores were much higher than Whites. Those who focus on these

23   R. J. Herrnstein & C. Murray, *The Bell Curve* (Free Press, 1994), pp. 548–9.

variations identified social origin and educational opportunity as the key mediators and the fact that IQ tests are inherently culturally biased. Despite the attempts of *The Bell Curve* to explain variations across population groups in America, it failed to deal with the fact that much of Black America is of mixed heritage. It failed to make a credible case that there was an existence of separate races and the belief that they have genetically different abilities.

Paradoxically, the idea of racial determinism persists on both sides of the colour line. For some people of colour it can be seen as a sign of 'lacking insight', a 'lack of racial awareness' or even treachery to suggest that 'race' isn't a useful way of describing Black exceptionalism. Let me take you back to my earlier observations about athletic prowess.

In my film *The Faster Race* for the BBC, I asked the question why so many 'Black' men dominated the 100m sprint in the Olympic final. Online we received a number of friendly observations and some sterner complaints about my conclusion that we were asking the wrong question. I argued the evidence suggested it was more to do with individual talent, motivation and aspiration than a group genetic disposition. I faced a howl of hurt from some Black people who felt I was taking away from the success of Black athletes, by pointing out their success wasn't a result of their 'Blackness' but rather their individual talent and the way they had chosen to develop those qualities.

There will be those of you who will continue to say, 'But hang on, Kurt, it is obvious people are different just by looking at the colour of their skin.' My response is unequivocal. How can it be reasonably claimed that this simple visible sign of difference explains everything, from behaviour and criminality to sexuality, employability and a host of other human traits? No, the response to that argument must be a resolute 'just because a person's skin is blacker than the next doesn't explain the genetic make-up of that individual'.

Genetic liberation

What the modern study of genetics has decisively shown is that by delving beneath the skin we are able to explain that perceptions of human value and quality may not be best identified by what we can see on the surface of the body. The clear biological differences between so-called races are so small and the evidence of intellectual superiority so wafer thin they are meaningless.

A confused biological determinism had long ago subverted critical thinking processes, unhelpfully mixing genes, physiognomy and culture. Phenoptypical features such as skin colour or nose shape are now regarded as superficial and irrelevant in judging the real nature and potential of human groups.

Geneticists such as Jones have identified that the key difficulty with the idea of race revolves around a lack of a proper understanding of the distinction between genetic variation in human populations, phenotypical differences such as external appearance (skin colour, hair type, nose shape) and cultural and behavioural characteristics as evidenced in belief systems, level of technological development or political organisation.

One thing that has struck me in my travels through Africa is that although a 'common sense' observation is that all Africans are black and have similar facial features, this is simply not the case. Skin shades are very varied, as is the colour and texture of hair, the shape of noses and even heads. In reality, the continent of Africa contains the most variation in physical and genetic types on planet Earth.

In genetic science this has led to the widely accepted conclusion that genetic variation within groups, that is, amongst the individuals comprising the groups (regarded in the past as races), is usually greater than the differences between the grouped populations. In short, racial variation is not helpful in understanding human differences.

Genetics and molecular biology have helped to show that race is only skin deep. Once you delve below the skin our similarities become all the more obvious. Ever more sophisticated scientific methods for seeing the human body have underpinned a modern paradox that race is a biological irrelevance, even though racism so obviously persists.

This must surely be a reflection that most of the language of 'race' remains anchored in what we have inherited from the past. But because of the enduring painful legacy of this inheritance it is proving difficult to accept that 'race' is a 'false reality'.

Culture over biology

One of the unintended consequences of the advance of genetic science is that our use of 'race' has retreated from a biological signifier into a cultural one. But cultural racism rooted in a similar determinism is unlikely to prove any easier to eradicate. After all, as we have seen, the 'history of race' has witnessed a transition from a religious, through an anthropological and imperial inter-pretation to justify a particular cultural system – one that as a modern society we are still trying hard to unpack.

As an undergraduate I was drawn to the writings of Frantz Fanon (1925–61). In his seminal book *Black Skin, White Masks*,[24] he argues that the colour of his skin effectively imprisoned him in a schema of some-one else's devising. The French colonial powers had used the evidence presented to them by Enlightenment

---

24 F. Fanon, *Black Skin, White Masks* (Pluto Press, 1986).

science to devise a cultural hierarchy where people of African descent (in Fanon's case on the Caribbean Island of Martinique) remained at the bottom of the social and economic pile, as it was in all imperial dispensations.

Fanon wrote, 'I am a slave, not of an idea that others have of me, but of my own appearance, I am fixed by it.' In a sense he was identifying the 'racial' dialectic, that the curse of racial domination is the condition, not of being Black, but of being Black in relation to the White. In other words, a cultural distinction.

People of colour living in the parts of the world that were predominantly 'White' have always faced micro-aggressions that become a form of enduring trauma as long as they persist. Fanon perceived himself to be cloaked in a skin that meant he was read in a certain way. And even now that the scientific evidence says otherwise, people – be they Black or White – are always struggling against that unconscious bias. It is this kind of frustration so described that I have found myself fighting against throughout my adulthood.

The point here is that it is what lays within that unconscious bias that is the problem, because these biases have travelled down the centuries wrapped in the certainties of a past and flawed science.

Fanon proposed that what was really needed was 'nothing short of the liberation of the man of colour from himself'. This is not a new idea; significant philosophers of colour, such as W. E. B. Du Bois in *The Conservation of Races*, suggested that whilst 'race' was scientifically problematic, it should nevertheless be seen as culturally significant. Writing in 1897, Du Bois said that people of African descent had a common racial ancestry because 'they have a common history, have suffered a common disaster and have one long memory of disaster'. It wasn't the skin colour that was important but what he called the meaning it brought with it of 'a badge for the social heritage of slavery, the dissemination and the insult of that experience'. What Du Bois was recognising over a century ago was that race has more to do with language and culture than biology.

I think the most compelling part of Fanon's argument is that 'race' has formed an intellectual prison, and has constrained our imagination, from which, despite the fact science has moved on, we still find it difficult to escape. We still ascribe meaning to race and that language continues to represent social relations between different groups of people along the colour line.

Can racism exist without race?

'Race' as an idea remains appealing in its simplicity because it is seemingly so observable. This has bestowed the concept with a sense of self-evident truth.

Nevertheless, as a constructed social category it derives its power from the powerful legitimation that 'race' categories have been bequeathed through centuries of repetition. As an explanatory concept it has proven remarkably adaptive to different environments and follows the flow of social change as stereotypes change.

Those who believe in 'race' as a key explanation of human variation would put to one side history, language and religion to suggest that there is something primordial or essential in our similarities at a genetic or bodily level. This has left us confused by the notion of 'race' but clinging on to old certainties, which in fact were never really certainties and only a way of preserving, as we have seen, cultural systems that had become a fact on the ground.

What this means in practice is that people have to be constantly educated to an appreciation of racial difference as there is nothing that intrinsically can make that difference obvious beyond skin colour. The trap 'race' springs is that we look to visual difference because it is the easiest thing to do. In our explanatory universe this has become part of a complex cultural system for identifying us as distinct from them, who is part of the club and who is not.

The paradox in modern Britain is that where there is a profusion of cultures and cultural mixing this simplicity breaks down utterly.

Ironically in British politics, 'race' has become a taboo subject, which means precious little advantage comes of remaining attached to a category that cannot deliver a change in the exercise of power in a reasoned public culture capable of simultaneously promoting both self and collective social development. It is not a sustainable association when the law and regulation begins to create a level playing field.

I am alive to the fact that by expressing an antipathy towards 'race' I could be accused of betraying those activists whose fight has been to secure equality of opportunity, equal rights and justice for people of colour. I merely observe that this form of political association has proven increasingly unstable and progressively unreliable as a means of achieving equality. Even Martin Luther King (1929–68) paid the ultimate price when he began to argue that justice and equality transcended race in the fight for political change.

The more sceptical we become of the status of easily visible difference, the more we shall be obliged to ask how a spectrum from human sameness to human diversity is to be calibrated. Indeed whether it has any intrinsic value beyond natural curiosity.

But racism begat 'race'. Racism is a rational outcome of the fear of what is different. Classifying that difference became 'race'. So, although 'race' may not exist in the way Europeans who first cast the scientific concept had it, the White supremacist ideas on which it was founded to explain the other have not necessarily died the same kind of neat death.

The fear of the other is both a psychological and a practical struggle that has exercised the passions, pretensions and politics of man. Having the means to challenge racist values or a White-supremacist, majoritarian mentality has been the real test of dealing steady death blows to 'race'. But to unravel this we need to untangle the mythologies and interests that many invoke to preserve 'race', despite their desire to be rid of racism. The two are symbiotic – one cannot live without the other but neither can they die alone.

To object to the use of the 'race' concept as an analytical tool is not to say that in promoting equality, justice and inclusion we should discount the potential consequences of its existence. Objecting remains an appeal to progressively 'de-racialise' our relations as we remove discriminatory barriers. We need to liberate our imaginations from all 'racialised' seeing and 'racialised' thinking that can offer only 'racialised' remedies.

From my earliest years I have been an inveterate watcher of mixed families on Britain's beaches. As a journalist I crafted that nosiness into a professional attribute. My fascination was particularly piqued by couples of mixed heritage and their children. With my childhood in mind, I wonder if and why we as a society oblige them to choose which parent's skin they should embrace in navigating life's struggles. Their dilemma is society's hang-up in a nutshell, forcing us to embrace and endorse this dialectic between racism and anti-racism as the basis on which our life chances are determined. We need to steer our way out of this orthodoxy that enslaves us with all its contradictions.

Part II:
Racist Britain?

'Humanity is waiting for something other than blind imitation of the past.'

– Martin Luther King Jr

I N PART I, I explored the provenance of the ideas, ideology and so-called 'common sense' surrounding ideas of 'race'. I argued that the evidence reduces 'race' to a bankrupt scientific concept. The past has nevertheless created a 'cultural system' underpinned by centuries of philosophical legitimation. Race remains a concept embedded in popular and academic debates exploring these cultural systems such as class, gender or ethnicity.

'Race' remains an idea with a vice-like grip on people's imaginations – we can't just wish it away. If it is a cultural system and cultures globally are both dynamic and different, we must try to be clear about how this differentiation explains our human condition. We should also expect ideas of differentiation to change where concerted efforts are made to challenge its discriminatory impact. Part II is about what the word 'racism' means in Britain today, a country where there is still abundant evidence that neither disadvantage nor discrimination have been eradicated.

Racism and denial in public discourse

If 'races' do not exist and, let's be frank here, very few people admit to being racists, why is it that British popular discourse is replete with allegations of racist behaviour or racism? Herein lies one of the central paradoxes of life in Britain. We live in a culture of denial that often encourages a genteel tiptoeing around the issue and has rendered politics stale and clichéd.

As Britain has seen a rise in new migrants, so the hostility to these particular migrants has shown that racism is no longer a condition that afflicts just the early arrivals from the Caribbean and Asia but also now those from Africa and the new arrivals from the eastern states of the European Union. So skin colour and physical difference are no longer necessarily the clear dividing line.

This has been followed by the rise in Islamophobia in the wake of the 9/11 atrocities and the London bombings on 7 July 2005, where Muslim communities have become 'suspect communities'. Terrorism seems to have reignited the anxieties that were in some kind of suspended animation after the riots in Bradford in 1995 and Oldham in 2001.

These civil disturbances have been characterised as responses to failed integration through the unsuccessful public policy agenda of multiculturalism, a policy framework that encouraged communities to focus on their distinctiveness rather than their commonalities. They also led to a slow drift in public debate away from what Trevor Phillips called a multiculturalism that had us 'sleep-walking to segregation'[25] and towards a greater insistence on citizenship, community cohesion and 'Britishness'. In this particular debate, celebration of diversity became a transitory empty vessel.

The hidden consequence of this shift is arguably a new kind of common-sense racism that positions asylum seekers, new migrants and Muslims as the

25 In 2005, former chair of the Equalities and Human Rights Commission Trevor Phillips suggested Britain was in danger of becoming 'racially' segregated.

enemies within. Combined with a greater awareness of this hostility, hate crimes reported to police services across England and Wales have been on the rise. Home Office statistics disclose an 18 per cent rise in hate crime offences reported to police in 2014/15, up from just under 44,500 to 52,000 incidents. Eighty per cent were classed as racially motivated and this contrasts with annual crime survey statistics that recorded a 28 per cent drop in hate crime over the past seven years. It's a confusing picture that suggests the boundaries and classifications remain uncertain.[26]

Over the past three decades the landscape of ethnicity (often used as a synonym for 'race') in Britain has shifted dramatically. Social analysts such as Victoria Redclift[27] argue that this changing social architecture of Britain has given life to 'new racisms'. But the arguments to explain these changes often reflect parallel narratives.

---

26 BBC News Online, 'Hate crimes reported to police up 18% in England and Wales', 13 October 2015.

27 V. Redclift, 'New racisms, new racial subjects? The neo-liberal moment and the racial landscape of contemporary Britain', *Ethnic & Racial Studies*, Vol. 37, No. 4, 2014, pp. 577–88.

These seemingly contradictory positions are part and parcel of the landscape of social change that fosters a culture of denial and hypocrisy over the issue of race and racism. Entrenched positions become new orthodoxies and 'you're either with us or against us' philosophies. The central question here that causes so much discomfort is how much is racism a part of that landscape, and if it is, how much harm does it continue to do?

At the same time, a parallel discourse has emerged supported largely by conservative political activists of colour such as Munira Mirza, who argue that we have entered into a 'post-racial' world where 'race is no longer the significant disadvantage it used to be'.[28] These commentators took as confirmation of this transformation the election of President Barack Obama in 2008. A triumph of wishful thinking over observable reality if ever there was one.

This counter-narrative goes something like this. Because of the super-diversity of some of Britain's largest cities, such as London, Manchester, Birmingham and

28 M. Mirza, 'Rethinking Race', *Prospect Magazine*, No. 175, 2010.

Bristol, dramatic changes in parliamentary representation, as well as the rise of economic success stories in minority communities, what we have is sufficient evidence to reveal that racism is not what it once was. It has broken down the traditional picture of BAME impoverishment and alienation as the only minority experience in Britain. It has given a certain salience to the Mirza proposition that 'race' and ethnicity are no longer inevitable barriers to success, with social class and individual character now the key variables of life chances in this 'post-racial society'.

Furthermore, those who believe racism is a thing of the past go on to claim that minority victimisation and discrimination does more harm than good and misrepresents the sources of disadvantage in modern Britain. This argument has led amongst other things to a growing clamour to recognise that White English victimisation exists and accusations that the White working class have been abandoned by the political elite and have become victims of a kind of reverse racism themselves. This latter argument is not new. The White working class have historically suffered disadvantage in parallel with new migrant communities. However, statistically speaking, it is certainly not a minority. Class is not colour-coded.

From convention to law in matters of 'race'

In a sense, there has never been a time when racism hasn't existed in Britain. As an imperial power this nation fostered slavery in British America and the Caribbean and then built an empire founded on the supremacy of the English.

The histories of British race relations and immigration have been closely interlinked, and shifts in the way policy-makers have dealt with people of colour has been mirrored by the path of academic discourse.[29] There have been three broad phases of change.

Premised on the existence of 'race', it has been the concerted attempts to deal with racism since the 1960s, through a series of Race Relations Acts, which illustrate

29 J. Bourne, 'The life and times of institutional racism', *Race and Class*, Vol. 43, No. 2, 2001, pp. 7–22.

the ebb and flow of the state's view on racism leading up to the Britain of today.

When I was a young boy dodging questions like 'where do you come from?' or 'how long have you lived here?', successive British parliaments debated how a growing sense of xenophobia against people of a different skin colour could be averted.

The law has long implied that 'race' is a secure means by which to define and differentiate between groups within the United Kingdom in the same way as it was in the British Empire before it. So, even though the biological sciences have of late debunked the concept of 'race', it is one that is broadly recognised in English law as a means of regulating conduct that arises from behaviour between people as if 'race' exists.

As always, conflict provoked change. The riots of 1958 in west London led to a lot of soul searching as these antipathies threatened to spill into major conflict at a time when businesses were busy recruiting migrant workers. The Home Secretary Roy Jenkins looked to foster a climate with the first Race Relations Acts in 1965 and then 1968 to promote 'equal opportunity accompanied by cultural diversity in an atmosphere of mutual tolerance'.

British policy-makers used these acts to promote a kind of informal policy framework of *'multiculturalism'* in an attempt to encourage giving these emerging migrant communities their 'cultural space'. Sometimes this allowed for greater levels of mutual understanding, most obviously through events such as the Notting Hill Carnival, organised by one community and enjoyed by many. It also fostered separate institutions with separate agendas that slowly but surely gave sustenance to a political culture of mutually exclusive expectations.

Whilst the first generation of migrant workers and their families began to settle, the children who attended schools found an education system that tried to squeeze them into a rapidly changing comprehensive model. This model failed to recognise the differences between existing social groups, let alone the new migrant groups. The results at school for White working-class children and migrant groups showed a widespread pattern of failure. The difference with some migrants was that their children were performing less well than they had in their original homelands.

In 1968, Enoch Powell jumped hobnail-booted into the debate on race in his so-called 'Rivers of Blood' speech. It is etched into my consciousness as a kind of political awakening. In 1968, listening to his speech made me feel vulnerable and indeed this translated quickly into phlegm in the face on the streets of London. He argued that a dramatic rise in the numbers of Black people would make it difficult to continue with the way of life England had come to know and lead to ethnic strife: [30]

> For these dangerous and divisive elements the legislation proposed in the Race Relations Bill is the very pabulum they need to flourish. Here is the means of showing that the immigrant communities can organise to con-solidate their members, to agitate and campaign against

---

30 The final passage of Enoch Powell's speech is the most renowned, delivered to a Conservative Association meeting in Birmingham on 20 April 1968. My grandfather, who was on the opposite side of the political spectrum, counselled me at the time that although Powell had great learning, he was a poor politician to predict a catastrophe that probably wouldn't happen. Finally, when I met Powell in 1991, I got my chance to test my grandfather's judgement!

their fellow citizens, and to overawe and dominate the rest with the legal weapons which the ignorant and the ill-informed have provided. As I look ahead, I am filled with foreboding; like the Roman, I seem to see 'the River Tiber foaming with much blood'.

That tragic and intractable phenomenon which we watch with horror on the other side of the Atlantic but which there is interwoven with the history and existence of the States itself, is coming upon us here by our own volition and our own neglect. Indeed, it has all but come. In numerical terms, it will be of American proportions long before the end of the century.

Only resolute and urgent action will avert it even now. Whether there will be the public will to demand and obtain that action, I do not know. All I know is that to see, and not to speak, would be the great betrayal.

In less than a decade, under pressure from a growing number of anti-racist activists, politicians from across the political spectrum realised that poor job and educational opportunities, housing and environmental issues meant the next generation, in other words the children of migrants, would 'grow up less well-equipped to deal with the difficulties facing them' and so would be disadvantaged. Compounded by clear evidence of racist policing, a discriminatory education system, a biased criminal justice system and unfair immigration law, fresh parliamentary debates led to a new Race Relations Act in 1976.

The overriding policy framework here was to introduce the concept of 'racial disadvantage'. It implicitly sought to tackle the disappointment and difficulties experienced by the first generation of immigrants and their British-born children. The disappointment was widespread and deep, the dream was that things would get better and they hadn't. There was a growing recognition amongst policy-makers that prejudice in and of itself was not the problem, unpleasant as it was, but rather acting out that prejudice leading to unfettered social discrimination was.

More civil disturbances in the 1980s,[31] saw Lord Scarman conduct a public inquiry under the keen gaze of

---

31 This was the era that prompted me to take up a career in journalism.

Mrs Thatcher's government. It recognised that more needed to be done to stimulate wealth creation in parts of Britain's inner cities which were balancing on the precipice of ghettoisation. But it was the reaction to the murder of London schoolboy Stephen Lawrence and the Sir William Macpherson Inquiry into that tragedy that cemented the idea of racism being at the heart of the British way of life.

On the release of his report in February 1999, the concept of 'institutionalised racism'[32] provided a new benchmark for recognising 'racial disadvantage' in Britain:

> For the purposes of our inquiry the concept of institutionalised racism we apply consists of: The collective failure of an organisation to provide appropriate and professional service to people because of their colour, culture or ethnic origin. It can be seen or detected in processes, attitudes and behaviour which amounts to

32 'Institutional racism' first appeared as a concept in the radical writings of US Black political activists Stokely Carmichael and Charles V. Hamilton in *Black Power* (Penguin, 1968).

discrimination through unwitting prejudice, ignorance, thoughtlessness and racist stereotyping which disadvantage minority ethnic people.[33]

Macpherson was the state recognising the reality of racism. Its legacy is much disputed, but in that historical moment it suggested that 'It is incumbent on every institution to examine their policies and the outcomes of their policies and practices to guard against disadvantaging any section of our communities ... There must be an unequivocal acceptance of institutional racism and its nature before it can be addressed.'[34]

Has this helped battle discrimination?

Having adopted an American model for 'racial' classification in the 1960s, Britain has continued to use this method to help root out discriminatory practices. The

---

33 The Stephen Lawrence Inquiry, Report of Inquiry by Sir William Macpherson of Cluny, February 1999, CM 4262-1.

34 Ibid.

logic is simple: if you know where the problem lies you can find a policy response to eliminate the problem. Despite it being far from that simple, employers, public institutions and the census all use ethnic or 'racial' classifications to identify different groups of people in Britain.

Quite often these categories are by degrees confused and confusing as they try to shoehorn individuals into categories that under close inspection lack rigour. Ethnic monitoring forms have a statistical purpose but they often offer more impressionistic categories than stable ones.

Self-identification is at the heart of the contradiction. I am of mixed phenotypological, genetic and cultural heritage. Genetically I am a mixture of English, Irish and West African gene pools, but was immersed in German and English working-class culture as I grew up. My three children are a mix of that and Anglo-Welsh ancestry on my wife's side of the family. It makes the point that the categories on an institutional classification barely do justice to the point of collecting the data in the first place.

If you work on the basis of the one-drop rule (which

nearly all my professional encounters have since 1985), I am referred to as Black. It is indicative that the key determinant for that classification is skin colouring. In reality, that is in fact a very poor guide to anything about me other than a phenotypological description of my skin colouring. Which, as most would see it, is not very 'black' at all.

The issue then becomes how do others relate to that label and how does it change their conduct and behaviour towards me? And in doing that, does it impact on my conduct and behaviour towards them and people who look like them. If looking at me is a poor guide to the kind of person I am and the qualities that I have as an individual, it is probably a very weak basis on which to make an assessment on how you should engage with me.

The school disco amply showed me the absurdity of these categories. I have two sibling cousins with whom I spent much of my teenage years indulging my passion for dancing. We regularly attended their school discos (a different school from mine) only to find me turned away at the door by a teacher who would ridicule the idea that we could be related and therefore I should be let in. Although our mothers were sisters, my colouring made a familial link hard for many people to stomach or even imagine. At more commercial discos, my older cousin, who was what one might today call 'fit', was often my dancing partner to the consternation of boys who thought it impossible for a White girl to have a Black boy for a 'cousin'. It was good for me, because I didn't have to share my family dance partner!

This captures in a nutshell the problem of unconscious bias that has for so long led to discriminatory practices and created a climate within which cultural racism can be underpinned. I believe my own example reflects the challenge facing modern Britain when it comes to trying to organise social policies around unsound categories such as 'race'.

The increasing educational, social, economic and cultural fragmentation of minority populations in Britain from whatever provenance (Afghani, Algerian, Bangladeshi, Caribbean, Chinese, Congolese, Cypriot, Ethiopian, French, German, Indian, Kenyan, Nigerian, Pakistani, Somali, South African, Ugandan as a non-exhaustive list) makes it difficult to see how such classifications can be of general use as a means of making rational decisions about public policy.

Whilst I might be arguing against these categories, in terms of investigating the nature of discrimination these categories seem to persist.

The British experience can be seen as something of a social experiment in historical terms. Although Black and White friendships and marriages are not new, they are increasingly unexceptional. Post-millennial Britain is a young, mixed society, which has inevitably had varying results and, despite some harsh critics, there are plenty of positives to indicate that it need not lead to the perennial conflict that Enoch Powell once predicted. I long ago concluded that my own encounter with Powell was a watershed because I understood that friendships, love, mixed living and working relationships were no longer anathema. Powell was wrong. What has transpired is that, when it comes to neighbours, workplaces and intimacy, there is a good story to tell. Discrimination now plays out in a Britain that is more at ease with ethnic differences. This is the multifaceted Britain that is hard if not impossible to simply paint with an abstract colour code.

Has Britain's accidental 'social experiment' made it a fairer place?

Since the late 1980s, Britain has become good at collecting data on difference. Nationally, we generate hundreds of datasets each year to try to track the differences in life experiences between ethnic groups. There are a lot of talented academics and commentators interpreting those statistics, so the purpose of this analysis is not to critique other commentators but to look at some of the hard data to reflect on whether the diversity in numbers is beginning to affect mainstream Britain in a significant way.

I contend here that there is a powerful narrative of failure projected onto BAME communities. Look at the questions that are most often asked about BAME social interactions and it will often start with the premise of some failure needing an inquiry. For some, these inquiries represent a Sisyphean burden of 'Blackness'. There is certainly a legacy of well-documented discrimination, but can we detect any winds of change? Is there any evidence that we are equipping ourselves for a 'post-racial' society?

Of course, looking at the numbers cannot always

tell you why differentiation occurs in the sectors I have selected to look at. Nor can data say whether ethnicity is or is not a barrier to advancement. But, demographically speaking, Britain is a far more complex society in its ethnic make-up than when statisticians started to collect the data just a few decades ago.

So does skin colour matter when it comes to affecting the life opportunities of people in modern Britain? The prevailing wisdom is yes it does, and it would be hard to argue it has no impact. The big question is how deep is that impact and is it endemic. Or, do we need to explore a different language for looking at the problems we face in modern Britain?

Who do we think we are?

Our baseline for identifying diversity across the UK is the British ONS census.[35] In 2011, it indicated that roughly 12.9 per cent of the United Kingdom population

---

35 Office of National Statistics, 2011 Census Data, National Identity by Ethnic Group DC2202EW, Nomis, 16 May 2013.

is BAME (Black, Asian and Minority Ethnic) and 87.1 per cent is White. In England, those proportions reflect a 14.7 per cent to 85.3 per cent balance.

We are a long way off from the American model of African-American, Polish-American or add-as-appropriate-American. Much of the debate surrounding ethnicity and identity in Britain is confused and unconvincing – although London may prove the exception to this characterisation. We remain some way off from an idealised 'cosmopolitan' identity.

Social attitude surveys often portray 21st-century Britain as a nation at ease with the idea of difference in a way neither the United States nor France is, even though there has been evidence of conflict in some particular parts of urban Britain. Since the 9/11 attacks, successive British governments have been unsuccessful in carving out a more cosmopolitan national identity.[36]

In official surveys of ethnicity in England, very few White people self-identify as British only. Rather surprisingly, around 14 per cent according to the census

36 K. A. Appiah, *The Ethics of Identity* (Princeton University Press, 2005).

see themselves as British only, whereas 72 per cent self-identify as English only.

When I was growing up it was common for people to question whether you could be Black and British, as it became commonplace to ask the same question of British Muslims post 9/11. It showed a clear ignorance of imperial history but was reflected in the Gilroy dictum 'there ain't no black in the Union Jack'.[37]

In 2011, there appears to have been a dramatic shift. Non-White groups (BAME) were more inclined to self-identify as British, discarding the idea that they are English. So around 43 per cent of African heritage, 55 per cent of Caribbean heritage and 72 per cent of Bangladeshi heritage record themselves as British. That presents an interesting picture, particularly when you consider that 61 per cent of White Irish say they are not British at all.

If ever it was, Britain is no longer either one nation or even the four nations of the Union. It has become a place of many nations and one where a significant minority

---

37 P. Gilroy, *'There Ain't No Black in the Union Jack': The Cultural Politics of Race and Nation* (University of Chicago Press, 1987, 1991).

is increasingly willing, prepared and able to pass with ease between them. There are millions of Britons in mixed families today. Divides along the colour line are being crossed every day in homes around Britain and that makes the notion of race all the more problematic in anything other than purely descriptive terms.

Employment

From the arrival of the ship *Empire Windrush* in 1948, which beckoned the modern history of large-scale migration into Britain, workers arrived from the Caribbean and countries such as Pakistan, India and Bangladesh with the desire to find the work that would make for a better life for them and their families. Idi Amin's decision to expel tens of thousands of 'Ugandan Asians' was perhaps the first mass migration to Britain where migrants entitled to British citizenship feared for their lives (of course, this does not include the hundreds of thousands of returnees after the end of empire). Nearly 30,000 Ugandans of Indian descent settled in the UK.

The primary challenge for these migrants and refugees

was in finding work commensurate with skill, getting fairly paid and being fairly treated. These of course became the drivers of the first Race Relations Acts against discrimination.

By and large, the jobs these migrants could aspire to were those not wanted by those already living in Britain. They were low-paid, insecure and in a comparatively restricted spectrum of occupations, despite some migrants having had a college or university education in their native countries.

Kashmiris went to Vauxhall in Luton, Caribbean Islanders to the factories of the Midlands and London, Pakistanis to the textile mills in Bradford and Lancashire, nurses into the National Health Service everywhere. No sooner had they arrived, though, than British manufacturing was hit by chronic large-scale decline and those workers found subtle glass ceilings in the UK prevented them from finding jobs in other sectors of the economy.

Inevitably unemployment rose quite dramatically amongst Britain's BAME communities and it became clear to many that better qualifications for their children born or raised in the UK would become a priority.

Barriers set in place by employers both in the public and private sectors as well as trade union attitudes and those of professional associations added to the cultural impediments to change in the workplace and these needed clear legal efforts to remove them.

Since the late 1990s, though, there has been a major transformation, especially for those who have sought to get themselves qualified. There is strong evidence that barriers to entry are being overcome even if discriminatory practices and unconscious bias still prevent progression. The most recent labour market statistics tell a varied story.[38] The figures for the past twenty years show a consistently improving pattern. This is important to recognise, particularly for anti-racist activists who can quite rightly point to enduring pockets of unemployment for poorly qualified minorities.

Importantly, the overall employment rate gap has gradually been decreasing since the early 1990s. In 1993, the respective rates were 51.9 per cent (BAME) and 68.7 per

---

38 Labour Market Status by Ethnic Group, Department for Work & Pensions, April 2015.

cent (White) and the unemployment rate also showed a significant differential in those last years of the John Major government – 21.8 per cent (BAME) compared with the overall population of 10.3 per cent. The employment rate for BAME in 2014 was 61.4 per cent compared to 73 per cent in the overall population. The employment rate amongst minorities has seen a greater increase than that in the overall population. The unemployment rate in 2014 stood respectively at 11.3 per cent compared to 6.2 per cent. There is still a significant unemployment gap differential between BAME and White but it is much lower that it has been historically. There is reason to believe this will continue to improve when we begin to consider the educational statistics later in this section.

Of course, these figures disguise wide variations within the non-White population. Those of Indian, Chinese and Pakistani origin (although not Bangladeshi) are now no more likely to be employed than the overall population, but there is a more consistent level of employment amongst all minority groups.

The patterns of employment have changed considerably, with employment by sector broadly following that for the whole of the British workforce. So whilst minorities are more likely to be employed in sectors relating to accommodation and food services, wholesale and retail trade, transport services and health and social work activities, there is a consistent rise in the numbers of young minorities entering into the professions and professional services.

There are also some interesting changes in youth unemployment seen in the labour-force figures on 16–24-year-olds. Although unemployment rates have consistently improved across all groups, it has improved the greatest for minorities and particularly Black young people. In a dramatic change perhaps encouraged by changing benefit rules, the numbers of 16–24-year-olds either in work or full-time education is now more or less consistent across the entire population at around 85 per cent, with the most significant increase amongst Black young people.

Improved education will bring changing opportunities. As long as we stay focused on eliminating barriers to entry to employment, this positive change should continue. Discrimination will not be eliminated, but discrimination on grounds of colour may well become more difficult to sustain.

However, we should never expect social transformation to be straightforward. Whilst the barriers to entry into the workplace appear to be diminishing, there is some evidence that employers remain resistant to BAME talent, that equality, fair access and treatment are not always *de rigueur*, and this could lead to a sense of graduate frustration and exclusion. If this were to continue, it could lead to civil unrest inspired by a graduate class.

In practical terms, it could also mean the loss of some of the best talent to other economies and the expansion of opportunities from the rising economies of the east and the United States where the popularity of British educated talent finds a berth in more flexible economies. The entertainment market in the United States, for example, has been a particularly fruitful one for some British BAME performers.

Of course, Britain has been in the process of economic transformation for over forty years, so patterns of employment would be expected to change, but for the purposes of my argument here the key change is that there is now strong evidence that school leavers from minority households are achieving consistently higher results in line with other groups and in some areas such as London are even outstripping White students. I shall come onto these education statistics in the next section.

There is now more BAME part-time working and self-employment, too, although the impact this is having on the wealth of minorities is not clear. So, for example, whilst studies show clear evidence of poverty amongst minority groups living in poorer urban areas, there is less information about the rising numbers of middle-class BAME who find themselves perhaps no worse or better off than their White counterparts. This was, for example, a trajectory adopted by the tens of thousands of Ugandan Asians, many of whom made their homes in Leicester or Southall amongst other places.

In London in particular, but equally in other big cities such as Birmingham, Manchester, Leeds and Bradford, the number of small minority-owned businesses is significant. Figures on this tend not to be comprehensive, but alongside considerable business empires established by South Asians there are many more Black-owned

Small and Medium-Size Enterprises (SMEs) than there were when I made a film for the BBC on the birth of Black businesses in 1998.[39]

The rate of growth has been significant and this perhaps partly reflects the ease with which business can set up in a deregulated economy such as Britain's. In 2012, it was estimated that 6.2 per cent of SMEs in the UK were led by an individual from a Minority Ethnic Group (MEG), contributing up to £30 billion to Gross Added Value in the economy (around 6 per cent of the total). In round figures this reflected the outputs of around 295,000 such businesses.[40]

Although there are some notable winners, there are still questions about whether self-employment is an automatic pathway to social mobility and increased affluence amongst BAME communities. But this is often a different question from whether skin colour

39 The BBC commissioned 'The Birth of Black Business' for BBC2's *The Money Programme* on the fiftieth anniversary of the arrival of the SS *Empire Windrush*.

40 Small Business Survey 2012: Estimates for Women-led, Minority Ethnic Group (MEG) led and Social Enterprises in the UK, Department for Business, Innovation and Skills, 2013.

is an impediment to progress and perhaps reflects the kind of lifestyle choice many British workers make.

One of the principal drivers for BAME entrepreneurs has been a way of escaping from the restrictions of the labour market, but one of the oft-repeated allegations for the brakes on entrepreneurial success was the lending practices of financial institutions.

A review of the academic literature on the subject in 2013 concluded that there was no evidence of 'racial' discrimination by the banks in not supporting MEG-led businesses. But it did highlight that these businesses disproportionately faced challenges that made access to finance more difficult, such as absence of savings, collateral shortages, poor credit-worthiness, poor financial track record or language barriers.[41]

A perception remains that discrimination exists and this lack of trust and confidence in sources of finance and mainstream support may have hindered growth in this part of the economy. But this is manifestly not the

41 Ethnic Minority Businesses and Access to Finance, Department for Communities and Local Government, July 2013.

same as arguing that the problem is being ignored, either by businesses, academics or government.

Sometimes it is important to say it how it is. Only a fool would claim that discrimination on the grounds of skin colour is completely absent from the modern workplace – or even that it can be eliminated entirely – but what is clear over the past two decades is that the patterns of employment have changed significantly and unemployment rates have declined overall. There is a convergence of the differentials between all groups in Britain.

What is important is that in the 16–24 school-leaver age group, big strides have been made in focusing young people's minds on preparing for the future. This is reflected in a far smaller proportion of minorities being left behind and far greater numbers – 3.2 million in 2014 compared with a shade over a million in 1993 – finding their way into employment in a much wider range of jobs (that compares with a rise from 24 to 29 million employed in Britain overall over the same period).

Of course, what isn't clear from this analysis is what kind of jobs and how well paid individuals are, but the key point is that barriers to a range of employment sectors are coming down and the efforts on the part of a younger generation are transforming their preparedness for the workplace. That is success.

Education

In relation to skin colour, my own experience of an English education was a mixed one. Certainly I recognise the analysis of many studies conducted in the 1970s of low expectations, but, since then, the statistics and experience reflect a dramatic change in both the quality of the experience of children and young people of colour and a corresponding transformation in the quality of the results being achieved throughout secondary and higher education.

My purpose here is once again not to deny racism exists (it is easy to find examples of where it does), but rather to point out the significant transformations that are being made. We must allow ourselves to believe success is possible. Racists who say people of colour are not good enough, and anti-racists who imply we can never be good enough for others, hand argument and victory to those who would oppress people of colour.

In the 1970s, children from migrant families were often doing so badly in mainstream school that parents decided they needed to educate them using the example in the Afro-Caribbean communities of supplementary schools. These were used to teach materials that didn't figure in school curricula as well as to stop a real decline in standards once children progressed from primary to secondary school. This included introducing children to the untold histories of Caribbean and African history. These were part of the broader British experience of empire and the activists felt this would encourage greater self-esteem so these children were better prepared to weather the hostility they encountered in secondary schools, where so many BAME children were failing.

In the primary system it was long held that children performed at a similar level irrespective of ethnicity. But once in the secondary sector, Afro-Caribbean children in particular fell off a performance cliff. It may have been low expectations of staff and parents. In my case, sport and drama were the areas where many staff had high expectations of me, less so on the academic front as I progressed through school. Few of my teachers would have imagined me ending up as a university professor.

Since I left school in 1980, however, there have been dramatic changes in the composition of the BAME population and also a transformation in the educational attainment being achieved by BAME pupils.

Curiously enough, the education system has always been resistant to collecting standardised data on ethnic minority performance for those under the age of sixteen, so it has often been hard to pinpoint poor performance, prejudice and discrimination other than in the anecdotal experiences of individual students. It has, therefore, been easier to identify and highlight failure than it has been to identify success.

In 2000, the performance of Afro-Caribbean students was giving particular cause for concern because it was considerably less than half the national average on exiting the system at sixteen judged by reaching five GCSE grades A*–C.[42]

---

42 Parekh Report, *The Future of Multi-Ethnic Britain* (The Runnymede Trust, 2000).

This was a persistent worry and it seemed to con-
firm that schools had low expectations and added little
value to this cohort's eleven years of educational experience. There is still some evidence that for a minority
of students, for example, with school exclusions data,
Black boys are disproportionately represented, but
on many other indicators there is reason to believe
BAME pupils are no longer affected in the way early
generations were.

At GCSE level, for example, the latest figures show
that a majority of BAME pupils now exceed the national
average of 56.6 per cent of five GCSE A*–C[43] (Chinese 76.4 per cent, Asian 60.8 per cent, Mixed 57.7 per
cent and Black 53.1 per cent). Only Black Caribbean
and Pakistani children lag behind, but the gap has been
reduced significantly for those two groups to around
3 per cent below the national average. Indeed, this
group is making progress above the national average.
Equally importantly, the variation is just as pronounced

---

43 GCSE and equivalent attainment by pupil characteristics, 2013–14, Depart-
    ment for Education, January 2015.

within the minority dataset as it is across the whole country.

This is certainly not conclusive proof that skin colour does not matter in secondary education, but it does suggest that these statistics reflect a dramatically improved pattern of achievement and that factors other than skin colour might provide the answer to why some pupils still lag behind.

One study focusing on London schools came up with a more intriguing interpretation of student achievement in the capital. When looking at White British pupils and their school achievement, the study noticed a greater degree of improvement in schools that had a mixed ethnic composition in London and Birmingham. The author concluded that:

> This is not by chance of course; a key part of the London effect is its attraction to migrants and those aspiring to a better life. More speculatively, because of a more integrated school system and because of a larger population of non-White pupils, more White British pupils have the opportunity for interactions in school with higher

performing ethnic minority pupils than those outside the capital do. This potential for peer effect spill-overs may cause higher pupil progress.[44]

This general picture of improvement becomes even more dramatic in higher education where statistics are more readily available. When I did my undergraduate and postgraduate studies in the 1980s in the humanities and social sciences, I could count on one hand the number of students of colour I encountered. This was certainly a product of a widening participation agenda, particularly amongst the new universities that joined a singular university academy by dropping the polytechnic nomenclature after 1992. Was this perhaps one of the unintended consequences of Mrs Thatcher's liberalisation of the university system?

Whilst there are significant differences between Russell Group universities and the rest,[45] overall numbers

---

[44] S. Burgess, 'Understanding the success of London's schools', The Centre for Market and Public Organisation, University of Bristol, October 2014.

[45] For example, in 2012, the London School of Economics had 4 per cent BAME British students entering compared with 28 per cent at Middlesex University.

going on to university are a far cry from my days looking for another non-White face on campus.

In broad terms, the latest figures from the regulator of universities suggest that minority students in all categories reflect a proportionally growing appetite that surpasses that of their White counterparts. Twenty-three per cent of university entrants in 2013 were from a BAME background, which reflects a year-on-year rise. That's around 356,000 students a year.[46] In another set of figures from UCAS,[47] which strips out the European Union students, the largest increase in entry rates to university in the period 2006–14 is shown to be amongst Black school leavers (Caribbean and African), rising from 21 per cent in 2006 to 34 per cent in 2014 – a proportional rise of 60 per cent. This should be big news.

Of course, it is impossible to predict the impact this will have on the economy, society and culture as a whole,

---

46 These figures are probably an under-representation of BAME students in terms of percentages because the figures for White students include those from other parts of the European Union.

47 UCAS is the University Admissions Service in England and Wales. UCAS, End of Cycle Report 2014, UCAS Analysis and Research, December 2014.

but it suggests nothing short of a tidal wave of ability and determination. Racism cannot keep back or keep down this many graduates coming onto the labour market without very serious consequences for social harmony. It would be a foolish waste of human potential and national investment.

There are other qualitative questions beyond these numbers, which still need to be addressed. For example, there are ongoing debates about how the curriculum might be reformed and who shapes the curriculum at the primary, secondary and college and higher education levels. It still largely remains the case that on these issues it is harder to argue that a form of monoculturalism doesn't still exist. In British schools you are still more likely to learn about the American heroes of civil rights than the important contributions made by Black and Asian people in the British Empire. For goodness' sake, Mahatma Gandhi was an imperial British subject, but British pupils are still more likely to study the significance of the American Wars of Independence and civil rights than British imperialism, the enduring consequences of British Slavery and British social transformations in the 1960s.

Historians such as Keith Jenkins[48] have long argued that no individual, group or institution has either the right or power to create a singular narrative of the past. And yet in schools and universities it remains difficult to identify where these alternative interpretations are being introduced into the curriculum. Britain's wealth and standing internationally cannot be divorced from its imperial past any more than it can from the cosmopolitan nature of its present.

Perhaps there is an obvious reason for this given that in the academic profession it is estimated that out of 18,000 professors in the UK only eighty are Black. Across British universities there are a paltry 7 per cent of professors from a BAME background according to the new vice-chancellor of SOAS in London, Baroness Valerie Amos.[49] Staggering as this statistic is, it is not easily explained by racism alone. The academy sees itself as a meritocracy and this hierarchy is graduated by degrees – literally. A PhD is a significant undertaking and the barriers to entry

---

48 K. Jenkins, *Re-Thinking History* (Routledge, 1991).

49 *The Guardian*, 19 July 2015.

are socially and financially high. In my case it was only a working-class grandfather who insisted a PhD was akin to a higher calling that made me stay the course. (Although I remain unconvinced on the higher calling point!)

There are still issues to resolve in terms of who gets the opportunity to progress through school and onto university; it is not as straightforward as saying there is always an issue of skin colour or cultural prejudice at play when progress is impeded in different parts of the educational sector. This is a sea change from when I began my university education in 1980.[50] A British education is once again something to be proud of.

Policing and criminal justice

Over my twenty-five years as a journalist, perhaps more than any other issue in British life, policing and criminal justice have occupied a disproportionate amount of my attention.

---

50 In 1988, I was one of the first British-born 'Black' lecturers to be appointed to the London School of Economics.

I often asked myself if I had been typecast into reporting stories affecting Britain's BAME communities, in particular the hostile relations between Black communities and the Metropolitan Police. But then that was one of the reasons I chose to become a journalist after the Broadwater Farm riots in 1985.

So, whilst members of the public would often ask me, 'Do the BBC only allow you to do Black stories?', and in all honesty it is a question I never satisfactorily answered, I was both pulled to these stories out of inclination and sent to these stories because of privileged access that I earned particularly within London's BAME communities. I know that my intervention on some stories made a big difference to the way they were initially reported, too, including the story of the riots at Broadwater Farm.

When I first started reporting from the Old Bailey and the High Courts, the only people of colour in either building were usually the security guards. In the courtrooms themselves it was effectively a 'Whites only' environment apart from the constant parade of minority defendants. It was depressing and hopeless. Then, a decade ago, I detected monumental shifts that couldn't simply be ignored. In 1987, Courteney Griffiths (now a leading BAME barrister) was junior counsel in the case that saw Winston Silcott on trial for the murder of PC Blakelock after the Broadwater Farm riots. In 2014, he was the Queen's Counsel leading the defence of a man accused of the same murder. This is emblematic of the personnel changes in the legal profession. When a BAME counsel defends White defendants, it is easier to recognise race is not the issue, justice is.

The police service is an instrument of the state. A police officer can not only curb an individual's freedom on the street but dramatically change their lives, including, in extreme cases, taking it away. No other officials have that power. The evidence suggests that the police service has historically allowed individuals with racist attitudes into the force and this has meant they weren't fit to be public servants.

The strained relations between police and poorer communities are well documented. From the Cable Street battles in the 1930s onwards, the modern police service has had a reputation for unfair play with working-class communities where dissenters took to the streets to voice their anger at being overlooked or, in the case of Mosley's Blackshirts, physically intimidated.

In the inner-city communities of London, Birmingham, Liverpool, Manchester and Bradford, poor policing practices have periodically led to rioting. I can recall the riots in London at the start of the 1980s when I was a student and the misreporting of those as 'race riots'. It perpetuated the myth that somehow this was a fulfilment of Enoch Powell's 1968 'Rivers of Blood' prediction.

Of course, it was nothing of the sort. Young people from all communities fought pitched battles with the police even though its harsh treatment of young Black men in particular triggered the disturbances. It was a similar case in the Southall march against the National Front in 1979, where teacher Blair Peach, a White New Zealander, was beaten to death by a police officer. In those days it was often difficult for some police officers to see beyond stereotypes and I too encountered the ignominy of stop and search on London's streets.

The strong levels of antipathy and distrust have

never been entirely dissipated even with a concentrated effort to change the ethnic composition of the officers policing our cities from an overwhelmingly White workforce to one more in tune with the communities they serve.

The 1999 Macpherson report was a seismic moment in British policing and one that has made everyone, not least the police, deal with the inertia in getting people to change their attitudes and practices so that skin colour stops being a basis for judging interactions between the police and public and by addressing recruitment within the ranks of the police service to promote more effective policing. One of the key successes of the Macpherson inquiry was to get British policing to recognise it had a problem.

When I interviewed a shell-shocked Sir Paul Condon for the BBC after the report was published, his barely suppressed anger at Macpherson's conclusions was obvious, but he did vow to set the Metropolitan Police on a new pathway to reform its culture and its recruitment. He insisted not all his officers were racists, a view which the evidence suggested was right, but he recognised that if the perception was that they were, all the work on policing by consent since the 1981 Brixton riots would evaporate. The Met needed to reflect better the diverse community it served.

So, in the Metropolitan Police Service, from a workforce that had only a handful of non-White officers in 1980 at the time of the Southall and then Brixton riots, the latest recruitment figures show that just over a quarter of recruits in 2015 will be BAME.[51] Overall, 11.7 per cent of current officers are from BAME backgrounds, which compares with 40 per cent in the London population as a whole. In senior ranks, the figures for chief superintendents and chief inspectors falls to 5 per cent.

The figures in London are significantly higher than in other parts of the country, demonstrating that this is still not a career path sufficiently attractive to BAME members of Britain's urban communities. In the absence of strong evidence that there is an active systemic barrier to recruitment, this can be put down to enduring

---

51   Figures supplied to Sadiq Khan MP by the Metropolitan Police reported in the *Evening Standard* on 9 May 2015.

levels of mistrust and high-profile cases of employment discrimination. In reality, this is not a job that many BAME individuals yet aspire to.

I have covered dozens of serious incidents involving the police, from the murder of PC Blakelock to the killing of Mark Duggan (both in Tottenham, north London) and the deaths in custody of Brian Douglas, Sean Rigg and Olaseni Lewis, amongst others. It is not only people of colour who have died after or whilst being challenged by the police; I also covered the disturbing inquest into the shooting of Scottish painter and decorator Harry Stanley when he was carrying a chair leg that was mistaken for a shotgun by firearms officers.

Without a doubt, the evidence in all these cases shows an enduring issue for some police officers when confronted by people who don't look like themselves. But a major ongoing problem for the police is the fact that grieving relatives have to endure a tortuous legal process lasting years to get close to understanding why their loved ones died. This process has probably done more harm to police relations with BAME relatives than any other, because it reinforces the perception that officers – and therefore the British state – will not be held accountable when they are responsible for the deaths of Black people.

Across the forty-three forces in England and Wales, 5.5 per cent of officers are from BAME communities, which has only marginally improved over a decade, up from 3.5 per cent in 2005.[52] Across the country there were 3.4 per cent of BAME officers at chief inspector rank and above. Only the West Midlands (8.6 per cent) and Leicestershire (7.2 per cent) had services with officer numbers close to London's.

If you compare these figures with the NYPD, which has come under serious criticism for its attitudes towards policing African-Americans, it is worth noting that non-White police officers match the White numbers overall and Black officers make up around 16 per cent of police numbers.

If we are striving to have a police service that represents the mix in the community and that continues to police by consent, then British policing has a long way to go to

---

52 'Police workforce, England and Wales', Home Office, July 2015.

catch up with America, although the evidence from there is that this may not stop allegations of rampant racism.[53]

Despite the improvements in recruitment and visibility of BAME officers, in Britain the police remain under suspicion on several fronts: deaths in custody, accountability and discipline, and stop and search.

Deaths in custody

Families like those of Sean Rigg or Olaseni Lewis have to endure years of wrangling to get the evidence before an inquest coroner to establish the truth of how their loved ones died. The system seems to place impediments in their way at every turn to prevent any disclosure that may harm the police service. When an inquest jury returns a verdict that says the individual died as a result of 'contributory neglect' by police officers, as in the case of Sean Rigg, it is hardly surprising that this becomes a matter of huge contention and more often than not a public relations disaster for the police.

---

53   #BlackLivesMatter

In the end this does not reflect the vast majority of the BAME public's experience with police officers, but if the most vulnerable are not safe in the hands of the police then people will legitimately ask if the service is hampered by individual racist officers or by an institutionally racist service, and whether either are fit for purpose.[54]

The Independent Police Complaints Commission has done little to help ease this conflict. Of all the public services, it appears that the police is the one where it is most difficult to get an admission of wrongdoing, even where there might have been a genuine mistake, and this continues to hamper the reputation of the police service despite the slow change in the police demographic. In my experience, this, more than stop and search, has become a major impediment to making progress on this front.

---

54 Sean Rigg and Olaseni Lewis both suffered mental health problems. Sean Rigg died in custody at Brixton police station in August 2008. Olaseni Lewis died at Bethlem hospital in September 2010 after a sustained period of restraint by police officers in the secure area of a mental health unit in south London.

Stop and search

The practice of stop and search still disproportionately colours the relations between young people and the police. Beyond school, a police officer is often the first encounter a young person has with state authority. For BAME communities, there is a history of unpleasantness and brutality in these encounters, although when you consider the miners' strikes in the 1980s it is obvious this equally affects other poor communities too. Changing this and the impact it has on public perception is a real challenge when most commentators acknowledge that it is a policing power that needs to be deployed to challenge crime and criminals.

There is abundant evidence of its excessive use against non-White people and whilst most public forums I have chaired on the issue recognise the importance of this power, it remains an enduring problem for police officers to sensitively carry out this duty out on the ground.

There is a strong argument that police need this power to do their job effectively, which is to deal with crime and criminals. It is not lost on people of colour that they are inordinately affected by the consequences of crime as victims.

In order to build confidence over its stop and search policy, the Metropolitan Police now issues statistics monthly. Over the course of the year to April 2015, these figures show that Black people consistently figure disproportionately in stop and search and are three times more likely to be stopped than a White person. By setting arrest rate targets (currently one in every five stops should result in an arrest), the numbers being stopped and searched may well have been driven down, but they are still staggeringly high in total terms.

For the year to April 2015, 162,700 stops were made in London, of which 61,951 were of people of 'Black' appearance and 22,503 were of 'Asian' appearance, of which around 21 per cent (Black) and 16 per cent (Asian) were subsequently arrested. That means at least 52 per cent of all stop and searches in the capital were non-White and the arrest rates were higher for non-Whites. We simply don't have enough evidence that these arrests were justified and until there is an adequate measure, deployment of the tactic and suspicion will go hand in hand.

Of course there is no way of knowing how many of these stop and searches are the same individual stopped multiple times or how many of the total non-White stops of 67,000 who weren't arrested were innocents going about their business. What the figures illustrate is the scale of the issue at hand, dealing with the bad faith this has helped build up over decades of poor policing practice.

But, again, and despite these considerable ongoing challenges, British policing is in a very different place from where it was at the time of the Macpherson Inquiry in 1999. This is largely thanks to cooperation between many volunteers and activists who have worked with the police to raise awareness and face the problems Macpherson identified.

The policing of the terror threat presents new challenges and has clearly had an impact on the perceptions in Muslim communities that they are a target for law enforcement. It is interesting to note that the stop and search figures of individuals of 'Asian' appearance are not currently disproportionate to their overall percentages of the London population.

Until 9/11, the principal tension in police/minority community relations was with young people of Afro-Caribbean and Pakistani descent. That all changed with the emergence of home-grown British jihadists and the threat of terror attacks. Muslim communities and individuals in Britain have found themselves under ever-closer scrutiny. Of course, this hasn't helped the old classifications and stereotypes one bit. Gone are the passive and docile clichés of 'Asian youth'; now it is assumed too that brown-skinned males with beards have suspicious murderous tendencies.

In fact, such is the plurality of those with a leaning towards jihadism that it defies skin colour coding. It rather subversively reinforces the point that 'race' is an entirely unhelpful way of trying to deal with the complexity of multi-ethnic Britain.

During my encounters with jihadists whilst reporting on terrorism, it is not the colour of someone's skin that has helped me decipher their objectives (that often remains impossible). Rather, it is their ideological/ theological standard that reinforces their similarities. So young British-Bengali men and women from Tower Hamlets, Muslim converts in British prisons or British-Pakistani men and women from Yorkshire have developed a separate group identity.

The policing of citizens can set off a chain reaction in their involvement in the criminal justice system and there is plenty of evidence over the past few decades that non-White people and the Irish (as a result of republican terror activities) have been treated differently at all stages of the criminal justice system beyond arrest.

But in the recent grooming scandals it is easy to see how we have become lost in the jungle of identity politics, where fears of causing offence have overruled the protection of the vulnerable. Was grooming of White girls by men of Pakistani origin racist or sexist? Does it really matter, if the failure of the authorities to intervene allowed the abuse to continue because they couldn't decide which 'ism' they were working within?

In 2000, the Parekh Report[55] found Black people were more likely to be charged and prosecuted than to be cautioned and sent to a crown court for a hearing. Black people were more likely to be acquitted in court, but if convicted more likely to receive a harsher

---

55 Parekh Report, *The Future of Multi-Ethnic Britain* (The Runnymede Trust, 2000).

sentence. Which meant Black people were six times more likely to end up in prison and for longer than their White counterparts.

The evidence from July 2014[56] is that a disproportionate number of prisoners, around 26 per cent of the prison population, were BAME, compared with around 10 per cent in the general population and of that nearly half are Black prisoners. In 2010, the Equalities and Human Rights Commission estimated that 'there is greater disproportionality in the number of Black people in prisons in the UK than in the United States'.[57]

The biggest shift over the fifteen years since the Parekh Report is the number of Muslims in the prison population, who make up more than 55 per cent of the minority prison population (although this will now be made up of Asian, Black and White inmates). It's easy to see from these figures that categorisation, even if only to collect data, can present problems of analysis

---

56 Offender Management Statistics: Prison Population 2014, Ministry of Justice.

57 *How Fair is Britain?: Equality, Human Rights & Good Relations in 2010*, Equality and Human Rights Commission, 2010.

and on their own these ethnic categories cannot possibly help understand why BAME individuals are so over-represented in British prisons.[58] This problem was exacerbated after the 2013 riots across the country.

There is still no satisfactory answer to the question of whether BAME individuals commit more crime, so it is impossible to draw any significant conclusions from incarceration figures.

The enduring issue with policing is that no matter how hard you try to train prejudice and misperception out of a police recruit, there is a danger that their personal feelings towards people of colour will have a disproportionate impact on that person's experience, if professionalism deserts them. If indignation and fear is what causes much of the damage in situations of conflict, then removing fear and indignation, for example with head cameras, might transform stop and search into a useful tool to tackle crime and reassure the public and stop it being a blight on BAME–police relations. You

---

58 Is an Algerian convicted of terror offences to be regarded as White, Black or Asian? How is this helpful to the understanding of the prison population in discriminatory terms?

can legislate for a change in law and practice, but the more power an individual has over another, the tougher the regulation over that behaviour needs to be.

Racist attitudes and racists undoubtedly exist in the police force and they won't go away just because we want them to. Whatever the reasons, it is clear that these attitudes are no longer sanctioned by the system itself. But when the state has the capacity to kill, it must be at its most unimpeachable in explanation. It is doubtful, however, that this alone accounts for the enduring antipathy towards police officers from all sections of the community.

Immigration

By its nature, the ways in which the government try to restrict the numbers of people coming into Britain are discriminatory. Since I started travelling abroad on my own in 1979, I have noticed that Britain looks very different when you come through passport control at Heathrow Airport. Once upon a time, passport control officers would quiz me on my travel details without fail and they would all be White. Nowadays, passport control is a reflection of the ideal-type rainbow nation.

The real question is whether Britain operates a Whites-only policy or whether it meets its international obligations in terms of migrants, be they sanctioned or refugees and asylum seekers.

Much of political debate on immigration is steeped in the language and prejudices that emerged in the 1960s, when large-scale immigration took place from countries of the New Commonwealth (as opposed to the White Dominions), both before and after decolonisation.

Such was the hostility to the SS *Empire Windrush* arriving in 1948, as the ship was entering the port to dock, that debates in the House of Commons actively sought to make a decision about whether the West Indian passengers (including many ex-servicemen) should be allowed to disembark. A Royal Navy vessel was even sent to accompany the ship into dock, much to the disgust of some of the ex-servicemen on the ship.[59]

---

59 From author's own interview with SS *Empire Windrush* crew member Peter Dielhenn for BBC London.

Of course, they did disembark, but they often found a cold welcome and difficulty in settling into the life they had aspired to in the Mother Country.

The series of race relations and immigration acts to regulate the numbers of non-White people[60] arriving in mainland Britain have always therefore been driven by debates about non-White people in post-war Britain. For the first sixteen years of my life, fellow Londoners were sometimes surprised to hear that I was born in London. When I travelled abroad it was even clearer that the image of Britain projected to the world beyond our shores was essentially a White one. A small anecdote should suffice.

In 1979, aged seventeen, I was encouraged by my parents to hitchhike around France to improve my spoken French. That it did, but it also introduced me to the French *gendarmerie* on a daily basis. Most of

---

60 Although Britain has always had a large number of White immigrants from Europe, the Americas and the former Imperial Dominions, these have never played as large a part in public discourse on immigration as the spectre of the rampaging hordes of non-White migrants 'swamping' or 'swarming' across UK borders.

these officers simply couldn't get their heads around my authentic British passport, believing instead it must have been stolen or forged. All to a man thought I was North African. A lot of that trip was spent listening to the technical conversation between them and their administrators over whether my passport could be real. Much of their vernacular is unrepeatable but it illustrated to me that Jeeves was still the abiding conception of Britishness. Still, thirty-five years on, I am rarely mistaken as someone from these islands, let alone born on them. I am more regularly assumed to be American. The 2012 Olympics offered a brief respite to such a blinkered view of Britain.

With the expansion of the EU and new internal migration rules since 2004, there have been greater numbers of migrants from our European partners, which almost match those from non-EU countries. In 2014, the figure for net migration into the UK was 318,000 (immigrants subtracting emigrants), of which 290,000 were non-EU citizens (including of course those from all the old Dominions and the United States) and 268,000 fellow EU citizens. It is noticeable, though, that the political debate quickly slips into talk of asylum seekers and refugees rather than French graduates, German corporate financiers or Americans. Last year, there were 31,400 asylum applications, which is a little under 10 per cent of the migration flow, but anecdotally this occupies a much larger amount of public debate on the issue of immigration.[61]

As a child, I always marvelled at how random strangers imagined that I was an immigrant and said I 'should go back to where you came from', whereas there was no such insistence for my German father, whose country had been at war with Britain just over a decade before I was born. It was clear to me by my teens that nationality and who we British were was firmly rooted in perceptions of 'kith and kin' as Harold Wilson once put it when deciding what course of action should be adopted against White Rhodesians who in 1965 made a Unilateral Declaration of Independence.

Only in the last few years have rights been equalised between a BAME migrant living in Britain who wants to bring a family member to join them and White South

---

61 Immigration Statistics quarterly bulletin, Home Office, May 2015.

Africans whose grandparents emigrated from these islands. This was manifestly a question of skin colour up until the 1990s – now they both have problems getting in!

But of all the responsibilities of government, managing migration is one that will almost inevitably remain riven with discrimination. But even here, this has become less of an issue of skin colour and more one of those who are here versus those who want to come here. That is undoubtedly why there appeared to be a popular paradox of BAME parliamentary candidates at the 2015 general election standing for UKIP. Whatever the political arguments are, the issue here is that skin colour is becoming a less than helpful guide in any part of the immigration debate.

Migration is an important topic to debate but so marinated is the discourse in the language of racism that it is almost impossible to have a comprehensive and objective debate about what is the right approach for the peoples of these islands to take. This is no longer a Black and White issue and yet we carry on our public discourse as if it is – to our detriment.

Britain is in denial that it is no longer the country it was and it cannot turn the clock back. Instead, it engages in a debate that illustrates frustrations of a lost past rather than one that wrestles with the problems of the present and future.

Culture, arts and the media

Of all the arenas in which people of colour have been able to demonstrate success and progress, the arts is a prominent one. There are so many prominent performers of colour who have emerged in Britain over the past twenty years that it is difficult to remember how it once was. For decades, only a handful got breaks and then it was often at the expense of demeaning roles such as the *Love Thy Neighbour* parodies of Black and White differences.

One of the nicer nicknames my peers had for me at school with my '70s Afro was Michael Jackson. Since then, a broad range of performers of colour have put 'Blackness' at the heart of popular culture. In a curious way, 'Blackness' is a positive enticement for the 'hard sell'. Pop stars and sporting icons adorn billboards and advertising spaces more than ever before and now

'Blackness' in this space does not put consumers off; rather, it sells an image of vitality and glamour that makes the stars into cultural royalty.

I have always been doubtful of notions of a homogenous Black culture that has, ironically, increasingly been projected by commercial interests to sell a lifestyle closely aligned with popular youth culture. There are those who continue to insist that people of colour are indelibly linked regardless of their wealth, gender, health, religion, political or ideological dispositions. Socio-economic differentiation within so-called BAME communities is paradoxically highlighted by the youth-oriented consumer culture.

In its broadest sense, culture is about identifying what Britain was, is and could be. Our interpretations need to be dynamic and not stuck in a dead-end conversation of biological determinism. Asserting that Blackness is a form of cultural superiority is another form of racialised biological determinism. So we should be deeply sceptical of racialised romances of sporting prowess and other such stereotypes.

One of the clearest examples of how this debate cuts both ways is in the stereotypes associated with high-performance athletes. When I made that BBC documentary on the sporting expectations for the Sydney Olympics (*The Faster Race*, BBC2, 2000), one of the most surprising criticisms of my conclusion that 'race' was a misnomer was the agonised responses from members of the public who were disappointed that I was challenging the idea that Black athletes had a natural superiority. It was as if I were removing a badge of honour of physical superiority which compensated for all the slights that Black people have had to endure.

It reminded me of the times as a young athlete when I was told that my African genes were the determining factor in my success, despite the fact that it was my English mother who had the sporting pedigree. This is why I find myself scoffing at the raciological mumbo-jumbo that is sometimes so casually and 'common-sensibly' dispensed as received wisdom.

I am all for success, but I am asking, what should success be attributed to? It is an argument used in popular culture to happily propagate the mythologies of 'race' through the celebration of sporting excellence to sell everything from sneakers to music. That's the way it is, but it unhealthily allows us to perpetuate the 'racialising' of popular culture, which in turn polarises and pollutes national debate.

There is a rich experience that the cultural mediators of our society should seek to interpret and which I would argue should reflect all the richness of those different experiences. I think it is of crucial importance that the debates about contemporary history, for example, should reflect the experience of all the participants in those events we choose to commemorate. The huge undertaking to commemorate the Great War of 1914–18 has in fact sought to recognise the contributions of soldiers from different parts of the British Empire who vastly outnumbered the soldiers recruited on these islands but who didn't fight on the Western Front.[62]

The national story in Britain is constantly being refashioned – that is the nature of culture in a modern, pluralistic society. There are real dangers that White

---

62 'Hidden Soldiers of the Empire' is an example of a public exhibition exploring these themes. It resulted from my work at Middlesex University collaborating with oral history champions Eastside Community Heritage and launched in October 2015 at the Bruce Castle museum in Tottenham, just a stone's throw away from where the riots of 1985 and 2013 took place.

people misunderstand why these stories matter. There is perhaps a fear that by highlighting untold histories somehow Britain will water down or minimise the contributions made by their own forefathers and mothers. An inclusive society like Britain needs a more considered approach to its diverse past. It is a question of recognising the experience and contributions of those usually omitted and understanding that the imperial past fashioned our cosmopolitan present.

The stories from across these communities are often intimately entwined, and an example of the benefits of recognising the various strands of experience that go to make a nation's story. In a country that now boasts millions of mixed relationships, this is common sense.

In the broadcasting industry, where I have spent the bulk of my professional life, common sense has often been a real challenge. Getting what are seen as 'minority' issues or stories onto mainstream television and radio has become easier, but it is difficult to make this happen more democratically if there are insufficient numbers of people who understand those alternative experiences working in the sector. This is one of the strongest arguments for making sure our broadcasting industry is staffed by a diversity of people.

I have always believed that the number of non-White people on screen, for example, is a false measure of change, given that it takes a much bigger team behind the camera or microphone to make the product. Far more funding decision-makers and gatekeepers need to come from diverse backgrounds, so that there is more competition for a plurality of ideas. This argument is at the heart of entertainer Lenny Henry's call for structural changes to the funding of television content.

When I joined the National Youth Theatre in 1980, it was a novelty to have one or two non-White performers in their midst. Now, thirty-five years on, this is no longer the case, and this is reflected across the piece in the theatrical arts. Access is now more competitive, but there are more ways to get a foothold in the industry, though, as in other workplace environments, many factors, including skin colour, can and will determine progress.

Research by Drama UK,[63] however, showed that

---

63 *Actors: The Real Employment Landscape*, Drama UK, November 2014.

there was an increasingly representative body of performers under the age of forty performing on the stage. Whilst television had just 4 per cent of performers who were non-White, in musical theatre 30 per cent were non-White and at the National Theatre 15 per cent were non-White. Drama UK pointed out that there were much lower figures for Asian than Black performers, but this may have more to do with career choice than discriminatory barriers to entry.

The changing perspective of Arts Council England, which under its new director Sir Peter Bazalgette has put diversity at the centre of the judgements it makes about the institutions and projects it funds, should help channel and monitor a more pluralistic approach across the sector rather than relying solely on particular minority-led arts groups to provide diversity.

But, at the same time that public funding of the arts has come under increasing pressure in times of economic austerity, the expansion of digital platforms of dissemination has made it clear that entrepreneurial artists are finding access to cultural markets much easier.

In the commercial world of book publishing, there is

clearly a bigger challenge as booksellers struggle to adjust to the demands of new technology that is disrupting patterns of production and dissemination and driving down profits. The Writing the Future report in April 2015 suggested that 'the best chance of publication for a BAME writer is to write literary fiction conforming to a stereotypical view of their communities, addressing topics such as racism, colonialism or post-colonialism as if these were the primary concerns of BAME people'.[64]

The report raised concerns that the publishing industry would find itself culturally irrelevant if it failed to reflect the growing complexity of its readership and, as award-winning novelist Aminatta Forna reflected, 'There is an orthodoxy whereby the presumed reader is totally mono-cultural, White middle-England.'

In a real sense, performers and artists no longer need to negotiate exclusively with gatekeepers to share either their craft or art. Some performers and artists have already been very successful in monetising their product using digital platforms and in areas like traditional publishing

---

64 Quoted in the *Writing the Future* report, April 2015.

which are slow to innovate, it may be that authors find new ways of disseminating their diversity of ideas.

It is certainly too early to tell how liberating this digital revolution will be in terms of the future plurality of the arts. But what is more discernible is that the rather restricted cultural discourses that have been the mainstay of the traditional media outlets are being challenged and disrupted by these new digital opportunities.

Where next?

The statistics paint a complex picture of modern Britain. It is no longer a 1960s Black and White story. Accustomed as we are to seeing real stories on the impact of racism on people's lives in the headlines, a broader sweep of the statistics indicates that there *is* a story about the improving landscape of a 'cosmopolitan' Britain.

It may appear to be a paradox that evidence of individual episodes of racism (in particular an increase in reported hate crime) persists, whilst at the same time there are improvements in the ability of individuals to harness opportunities and transform their lives irrespective of skin colour. The real issue is that both conditions exist in Britain. Just because racism affects some people's lives doesn't stop others finding they can make the best of their talents and thrive in a more inclusive society.

This is my argument. I believe we have to go beyond the set beliefs and old campaigns, which did so much to challenge the foundations of racism, but at the expense of consolidating notions of race and fostering a crude politics of identity. Identity politics has taken the optimism of multiculturalism up a political cul-de-sac.

We have moved a long way from the Britain of my childhood, where just about every walk of life saw systemic barriers to entry for people of colour. But just because we might argue Britain is a fairer country than it was when I was growing up, that doesn't mean there isn't widespread unfairness or injustice. Just because it is a more inclusive and equal society, doesn't mean there isn't still widespread inequality. What is changing in an observable way is that skin colour is not always the key determinant of life's fortune and misfortune.

To where exactly do we hope to proceed by holding onto categories that ethically, intellectually and analytically we recognise are increasingly bankrupt? Categories that we hold onto only because we are too lazy to create a more accurate and dynamic narrative, lest it undoes all the good work that is publicly or privately resourced under the 'racial' rubric.

In the United States, the civil rights movement has experienced a similar dilemma. From emancipation in the 1870s, oppressed Americans and their supporters developed strategies of survival and patterns of adaptation to centuries of discrimination and exclusion that have become increasingly unsustainable in what we might call a *politics of modernity*.

Finally, there is, I believe, a real danger that we allow identity along colour lines to become wrapped up in victimhood. The image of the victim can be useful but can also obscure the moral and political questions arising from the demands for justice. Justice is a generalised and universal concept and cannot be particularised to a specific group, however determined that is.[65]

---

65 For a more detailed exploration of these themes see O. Patterson, *The Ordeal of Integration: Progress and Resentment in America's 'Racial' Crisis* (Civitas Basic Books, 1998).

The role of victim has serious drawbacks as the basis for political identity, as James Baldwin (1924–87) put it:

> I refuse absolutely to speak from the point of view of the victim. The victim can have no point of view for precisely so long as he thinks of himself as a victim. The testimony of the victim, corroborated, simply the reality of the chains that bind him – confirms, and as it were, consoles the jailer.[66]

I believe it is fair to argue, as I have done here, that BAME Britons are now very much part of the nation's political life, in Parliament and local government. The recent intake of forty-one Members of Parliament shows this goes well beyond tokenism and a primary focus on BAME representation.[67] In 2014, across local authorities in England including the London Assembly, 4 per cent of elected representatives came from

---

66 Quoted in P. Gilroy, op. cit.

67 A lot of lobbying work by Operation Black Vote, founded in 1996 and led by Simon Woolley, established the principle that opening up access in Parliament meant across parties of all political persuasions.

a BAME background. In London, the figure rises to 16 per cent BAME councillors. This is a sign of a successful transition.

This success appears to run counter to the fear that the fragmentation of the 'Black vote' will diminish representation. How could you be a Black Tory without being a traitor? How can you be a Black Republican presidential candidate in all good conscience? How can a Black person be in the Front National in France or UKIP in Britain? The fear presupposes that at the heart of a political movement is a sense that there is a common search for the truth that drives them. Do such 'Black truths' exist and provide a basis for mainstream political action? Can BAME leaders be genuinely inclusive if they are driven by deterministic colour-coded politics?

I am suggesting that political argument and the policy-making remedies are increasingly subject to open discussion and should not be trumped by skin colour and codes of conduct that are ascribed deterministically to that skin colour or other inherited characteristics. Put simply, we must stop assuming and insisting that people join a particular political struggle or must hold particular views because of the colour of their skin, their cultural heritage, a particular history or some robustly asserted received wisdom.

The role of BAME performers, artists and sportsmen and other key players is being transformed, school achievement is increasing year on year and university enrolment even amongst the poorest represented cohort (Black male school leavers) is no longer a failure. It is fast becoming the norm that not a single British university today is an all-White bastion, although progress towards diversity in some institutions remains gradual.

We cannot dispute the fact that low incomes, child poverty and crime remains an enduring problem in poor communities in which BAME families are significantly represented. We simply don't know whether this is a question of skin colour as opposed to other factors that account for all those people who shoulder the burden and misfortune of impoverishment.

The statistics I have explored (and there are many more) suggest we have approached the limits of broad-based politics defined singularly by an anti-racist agenda.

But now that struggle has delivered real advances, it has sprung a trap from which we are finding it difficult to escape. In the end, persisting with this narrative without a meaningful corrective could spell disaster for the self-belief and progress of the majority of BAME young people who are proving by their actions that they have reservoirs of talent equal to any of their peers. Worse still, identity rhetoric that focuses on race-conscious politics and BAME exclusivity may play straight into the hands of the bigots and forces of reaction they have so ably opposed since the 1960s.

At the heart of my argument is a realisation that 'race' isn't scientific truth, it exists only in our imagination. If we wanted to un-imagine 'race', we could. We can continue a process of re-education in schools, universities and in the media, which has started to take root to transform British society from one built on racist assumptions to one aspiring to inclusivity and a 'cosmopolitan' set of values.

If we want to fight persistent racist attitudes, we need a critical politics against racism, oppression and prejudice that cannot be channelled, underlined and emboldened by a continuous invoking of 'race' as the ultimate arbiter of political truths.

Millions of people have demonstrated they want to live this change, with the rejection of colour lines in their own families. Ultimately, the remedies to inequality, injustice and discrimination are to be found through open politics that is not governed by 'racial truths' – and we should not fear saying so.

Part III:
Imagining Beyond 'Race'

'What we need is a great big melting pot. Big enough
to take the world and all it's got and keep it turning
for a hundred years or more and turn out coffee-
coloured people by the score.'

– Lyrics from 'Melting Pot' by Blue Mink, 1969

S O FAR IN Parts I and II, I have explored the 'roots of race' and presented evidence which challenges the idea that racism remains an all-encompassing experience for people of colour in Britain or that 'race' is the key explanatory concept to explain all disadvantage and social interactions between people with different skin colours.

In Part III, I want to ask if it is possible for Britons to wean themselves off the habit of 'race-thinking' and reimagine a Britain beyond race. Is a cosmopolitan identity possible?

The ontology of race has fixed our gaze on what Du Bois referred to as 'color, hair and bone' and from that built an epistemological approach that is fraught with contradictions. 'Race' has become the imperium for false prophets.

For much of its history, 'race' has mattered too much

and often for the wrong reasons. As a 'signifier' it retains residual political meaning. But in this book I have argued thus far that this has always been fluid, and we should expect its meaning and impact to change as circumstances in the world around us change.

This reasoning makes sense to me both from my own personal experience and intellectually. One incident in particular early in adulthood drew me towards this position. On 9 July 1982, my cousin Keith, to whom I was very close, was murdered in Hertfordshire. To this day, the crime remains unsolved. He was killed after being repeatedly stabbed on the high street of the small town of Broxbourne whilst he was riding his bike home. He was twenty-seven. The incident took place outside the local police station. Like many young people, he was distrustful of the police, and it is quite possible he decided not to seek refuge in the police station because of this, though we shall never know.

Keith's savage murder, without apparent motive, was an unmitigated tragedy for our family. Because of my skin colour, when I recounted this story of personal loss, people would often lament it could so easily have happened to me. That was true, but not for the skin colour reasons they often assumed in roughhouse Britain. The difference between Keith and myself was he was White. His murder had nothing to do with skin colour and everything to do with unadulterated violence perpetrated, we can only assume, by someone with psychopathic tendencies. The point of this story is that it has always given me pause for thought in my interpretation of events I have reported on, that in Britain we can all be victims and skin colour will not always be the cause of it.[68]

A 'race-thinking' cul-de-sac?

When I was eight, the British pop group Blue Mink, fronted by American singer Madeline Bell, had a massive

---

68 In so many words, Keith and I often talked about the question of colour, difference and identity. Our mothers are sisters. I was twenty when he was murdered and he was as clear-sighted on this as I was. As an artist he captured this in two self-portraits. One of himself as an ordinary English boy and the other as a dark-skinned version of himself, cleverly disguised in green rather than black pigmentation. Another painting of me alone on a yellow brick road I have interpreted as his depiction of the lonely journey I would have to take to discover the identity answers for myself. I have sorely missed his company on that journey.

hit with the song I drew on at the start of Part III. It is a song I sang at the time with such gusto that it has been committed to memory to this day. It is a song of hippy optimism!

What appealed to me in my innocence was its conception of a world in which 'race' became meaningless, because everyone would look like me. It was this outlook that encouraged me to invest my sense of identity in a cosmopolitan set of values that reflected the true diversity of my upbringing.[69] I came progressively to see that I was more than the sum of my cultural parts.

In his study *Race: A Study in Superstition* (1937), Jacques Barzun[70] (1907–2012) introduced the idea of 'race-thinking'. He argues, quite persuasively in my view, that in the absence of a biological justification, this simple notion explains how 'race' is commonly deployed in social and cultural relations. Here, in essence, is what Barzun asked the reader to consider.

---

69 For a fuller discussion of cosmopolitanism see K. A. Appiah, op. cit.

70 For a fuller discussion of the importance of Jacques Barzun see J. Downing & C. Husband, *Representing 'Race': Racisms, Ethnicities and Media* (Sage Publications Ltd, 2005).

Race-thinking is a habit not confined to those scientists and politicians who create systems or preach discrimination, and can be said to occur whenever an individual in conversation implies the truth of any of the following propositions. First, that mankind is divided into 'pure' or 'mixed' races distinguishable by physical features transmitted 'through the blood'.

Secondly, that the intellectual and moral behaviour of human beings can be satisfactorily accounted for and related to a physical structure denoted by the racial label. And, last but not least, that all of individual personality, ideas and capacities, national culture, politics and morals, are the products of signifiers such as race, class, nation, family, and nothing more needs to be determined to establish the causality between these signifiers and the spiritual output.

Sometimes these three types of race-thinking are indistinguishable one from the other. Each one of these is sufficient to evoke the veracity of the idea and they are willingly used interchangeably in all walks of life. Race-thinking is something I have instinctively resisted since childhood, often to my own detriment.

Barzun is describing 'race-thinking' as an intellectual tool, using 'race' as a descriptive and explanatory concept. Through this pattern of thinking, all human variation is reduced to one stable variable associated with an individual, namely their 'race'. Reference to 'race' therefore trumps any other explanation for complex social relations. Without the whiff of plausibility, however, 'race-thinking' would not have been so resilient. The aphorism 'Is it because I is Black?' is surely the reflexive response to an idea that for too long has prevailed in capturing a multitude of social and political circumstances.

The notion of 'racialisation' goes a step further to explain the process by which commentators extend 'racial meaning to previous racially unclassified relationships, social practice or groups'.[71] Combining 'race-thinking' and 'racialisation' illustrates how the mythologies surrounding race and racism can be perpetuated in a world where public debate is dominated by the media.

---

71 M. Omi & H. Winant, *Racial Formation in the United States* (Routledge, 1986), quoted in M. James, 'Race', *Stanford Encyclopedia of Philosophy*.

In this sense, the media has helped create, foster and stabilise the use of concepts that are otherwise redundant. It creates from myth a sense of reality. Employing 'race' as real, whether in the news agenda or entertainment, is to participate in this idea of 'racialisation' – it is effectively a production line of 'race-thinking'. The mythology isn't a truth, but the ideology of 'race' supports the myth and so it has become accepted as a common-sense reality over time.

In British politics, for example, the word 'immigrant' has a decades-long history of being 'racialised', even though as many White people have migrated to Britain as non-White, but non-White migration was presented as the problem. We live in a world where competing meanings of 'race' make the observable realities of racism complex, multi-layered and ultimately confusing.

It is difficult, therefore, to see how any attempts to de-racialise debates can be achieved without the media, in particular, presenting alternative narratives that challenge the dominant social and political values which have come to regard 'race' as a key way of differentiating life chances and isolating disadvantage.

Changing the way we see and reflect ourselves

In October 1985, I was just about to take up a scholarship to undertake doctoral studies at LSE. Despite wanting to be a journalist, it was a temptation I found hard to resist. No one in my family had ever been within touching distance of this kind of academic achievement and I could barely believe it myself.

The same month, I stumbled into the Broadwater Farm riots after dropping my brother-in-law Simon off after a day out. He was living close to the junction where the rioting on the estate literally exploded with the first Molotov cocktails. That evening's BBC news broadcast looked like Armageddon. Simon's flat was under threat of being burned out as cars were set alight underneath his bedroom window. People had to cover their faces with wet blankets so as not to be overcome by the fumes. Racing back to Tottenham that night to try to rescue him was the stuff of living nightmares as the whole area had been cordoned off. Happily he survived to tell the tale, but moved out shortly thereafter. The mental scars of that night will never leave me, however.

Over the next few weeks, the coverage in the newspapers and in the national media convinced me that I should become a journalist. And, although I delayed that decision until I had completed my doctorate in 1989, the experience would stay with me for my entire twenty-five years at the BBC. In fact, my final news report for BBC News in 2014 was on the acquittal of Nicky Jacobs for his alleged involvement in the murder of PC Keith Blakelock at Broadwater Farm. Life came full circle.[72]

The media has a responsibility not just to preserve open debate but to help constantly reinterpret what is mainstream in our society. But for many years representation of difference and the dynamic way in which different communities interact over time was not reflected by the British media. One of the key obstacles was that the cultural change needed within media organisations could happen only if they recruited beyond the social groups from which they had always traditionally done so.

---

72 In 2005, I made the definitive documentary for BBC2 on the Broadwater Farm riots, *Who Killed PC Blakelock?*, which won praise from all sides in those disturbances.

There existed in the BBC, for example, a kind of professional homogeneity that was obvious to any person of colour working for the BBC. In the 1990s, that representation of diversity on screen was a function of the organisational and employment issues off screen. Fair representation becomes a victim of groupthink when decision-makers share a particular way of thinking. Change requires different types of people as well as a broader range of mindsets. Difference can be shown partially through the faces of the presenters and reporters on screen, but also more effectively through the plethora of experts and performers who appear in the media to animate the debates and desires of mainstream society. In the end, Oxbridge networks are valuable for the individuals but very tight and often inward looking. This does not serve an open culture well. This was one of the objectives of *Black Britain*, a series that ran on the BBC for several editions and in which I played a proud reporting role.

I began working at BBC London in 2001 shortly after Greg Dyke described the BBC as 'hideously white'. To be fair, most of the White people were not hideous, but often they were closed off from the experiences of minority communities.

Certainly, the gatekeepers who had the ability to transform opportunities and change agendas remained very White, and the BBC has spent a lot of energy in trying to address this, often quite unsuccessfully with dozens of minority-focused initiatives. More recent initiatives launched in 2014 under Tony Hall have a better chance of working because there is now a stronger cohort of a mixed talent base to take up the challenge. But the BBC is not immune to the broader changes in the industry, and tackling these remains an institutional priority. This has often meant that those who do break the White, male glass ceiling end up aping the cultural attitudes to survive.

The media is changing. New technologies, globalisation and shifting social expectations are leading to massive rethinking and restructuring. This is captured by economist Joseph Schumpeter's (1883–1950) notion of *creative destruction*.[73] As the media industry

---

73 J. A. Schumpeter, *Capitalism, Socialism and Democracy* (Harper, 1943).

innovates in responding to new technologies, the old means of production and distribution break down and make managing change extraordinarily difficult. It is not obvious who the winners and losers will be.

What kind of national and community conversations will we be having in ten years' time? What is clear is that the emerging digital platform has unleashed a wave of creative innovation. In terms of its impact on the debates about diversity and difference, it has enabled a more plural discourse that is critical of the mainstream media and this is changing the way in which our differences or, indeed, similarities are presented.

As a journalist, it was always my experience that the mix and expectations amongst my audience were ahead of those who were making taste decisions within the BBC. Ultimately, it is a conservative organisation and change happens slowly. Broadcasters are no longer the principal gatekeepers for audio-visual content.[74] So much content is now available online that audiences

---

74 There are of course questions over the trustworthiness of sources, but this is another debate entirely.

have access to alternative narratives, interpretations and representations that challenge our normative understandings of difference.

This is a form of intense 'creative disruption', where, for example, BAME media people can present how they see themselves to an audience rather than relying on how others see them, and other viewers of the content can freely challenge comments on any particular posting. Facebook is littered with examples of ordinary people not standing on ceremony or using 'racial solidarity' to ignore or defend bad behaviour. These creative interventions reflect a very different view of representation that often makes the mainstream players appear timid, out of date and uncompetitive.

Whilst more research is needed to understand what new norms might be emerging, it is fair to say the sights, sounds and cultural challenges of the internet space will have a dramatic impact on the issue of difference and 'race codes'. The 'news feed' on Facebook alone presages such a revolution of the collective imagination.

There are many astounding examples of this 'creative

disruption'. Think about how mobile-phone videos are transforming the debate on police shootings of civilians in the United States. Citizens have been able to disseminate information in real time and challenge the establishment view. In the case of police shootings, such pressure has even shown the establishment in the shape of the FBI doesn't have the facts to take a view.

Very little research is yet available on the impact of this new exposed face of policing on police policy and procedure, but it cannot be long before such digital representation will begin to change people's perceptions of the world they and their fellow citizens live in. It has left a policing culture of denial beleaguered.

The events of 9/11 and the emergence of radical Islamists have had a dramatic impact on the representation of the Muslim community in Britain. Whereas the news gatekeepers had begun to recognise the bias in representation of people of African descent, it took some time to recognise the impact of using inaccurate and emotive language which implied Muslims and terrorist outrages were synonymous, or that fundamentalism and Islam were natural bedfellows.

It is the easiest thing in the world as a reporter to rely on cliché and stereotype when you are rushing for a tight deadline and you have few words to express yourself. I tried very hard over many years to avoid such clichés when reporting on terrorism, street-gang violence or refugee and migrant issues.[75]

It remains the case that most journalistic mainstream enterprises are still very poor at recruiting BAME staff. The difference is that now there are new opportunities for people to represent themselves and their lifestyles on social media and other platforms offered by the expanding digital landscape.

Whilst a lot of what appears in online videos can be nonsense, biased and reflect long-standing prejudices, there is also plenty of opportunity to hear and digest alternative currents of thought on any given issue. There is a kind of democratising power in being able to ignore

---

75 In fact, over the course of my career I won more Race in the Media awards (run by the Commission for Racial Equality) than any other individual British journalist. I think that had a lot to do with my sensibility towards the way in which I portrayed people of colour in my stories and the range of stories that I was able to get into the mainstream news output.

the mainstream outlets to tell your own story from the digital platform offered by the internet. The more video content that is presented on social media platforms, the more difficult it is for the mainstream media to ignore alternative representations.

Believing in ourselves, or the myths created about ourselves?

I start from the controversial position that everyone, including the victims of racism, can be racist. I believe there is a real danger that we become so thoroughly cloaked in the garb of the eternal victim and White people in the role of eternal oppressor that we cannot recognise genuine progress and concentrate our efforts to focus hard on those places where disadvantage and racism continue.

The first Race Relations Act (1965) set about trying to eliminate the racist behaviour of a host community that had to absorb people from a rapidly disintegrating British Empire, where the attitudes of racial difference and inferiority had not been discarded.

The legislative changes set about trying to level the playing field in housing, employment, education and public services. It did so by attempting to change the behaviour of decision-makers to remove the barriers to fair treatment on the basis of skin colour.

When this arguably failed to address the lot of migrant communities and their children, public disorder followed. It was then recognised that greater emphasis needed to be placed on changing the life aspirations and opportunities of the children of migrants. It is perhaps a universal truth of parenting that however hard it is for one's parents to survive and fight injustice, children think and behave differently. In short, my generation demonstrated that they were here to stay and were not prepared to endure the casual humiliation, lack of opportunity, and indignity often visited on our parents' generation.

In Britain as in America (and other parts of Europe that had colonial possessions), the patterns of discrimination and the language of 'race' have been stubbornly resilient despite the fact that a good deal of progress has been made.

There is little doubt in my mind that though Britain still has to achieve greater equality and enable diverse people to prosper, any ideas of national purity are pure fantasy. We have travelled a long way since I sat in that bicycle seat and felt I was so disliked simply because of the colour of my skin.

Attitudes across the colour line have been radically changed by millions of British families where parents or grandparents were 'foreign'-born but have melded through personal choices and histories into families that were born on these islands.

I am often struck how much more optimism there is amongst ordinary British people as opposed to those who choose to lead us and allow themselves to be so pessimistic about where Britain is heading in its cultural mix. I would argue that the row over the winner of the 2015 BBC *Great British Bake Off* title, Nadiya Hussain, is a sign of this tension. On the one hand, the winner felt that her success was a sign that the audience was more accepting than she thought they would be of her cultural particularities as a headscarf-adorning Muslim and made her feel comfortable with her success.

'I wasn't thinking about representing Muslims, I was thinking about my bakes … It's nice to be on a show where your skin colour or religion is incidental.'[76]

But certain commentators chose to see her win as a sign of political correctness at the BBC and not the triumph of talent. I have long argued that the more BAME people we have shaping our national narratives the sooner we will be more comfortable in our own skins. It is tiring and patronising to be told the triumph of your own talents belongs to others. I know, I have been told this to my face many times.

However much we as a society like to dwell on our false image of a monocultural past – the revival of studies of empire[77] are a counterbalance to this – there is no turning back, and coming to terms with the consequences of this past will offer us a new balance. 'Increasingly the British are beginning to appreciate that imperialism was not just something "we" did to other people

---

76 Nadiya Hussain, quoted in *The Guardian*, 13 October 2015.

77 For example, T. Hunt, *Ten Cities that Made an Empire* (Allen Lane, 2014); K. Kwarteng, *The Ghosts of Empire: Britain's Legacies in the Modern World* (Bloomsbury, 2011).

overseas, but a long, complex process that transformed the culture, economy and identity of the British Isles.'[78]

The more 'race-thinking' we indulge in, the more racism becomes all encompassing. In the end, this can only trap us in a paradigm from which it becomes increasingly difficult to escape. It works against the principles of an open society and 'racialises' the essence of humanity itself.

But, equally, we are not obliged to fall for a new mythology of a 'post-racial society' in which racism has been slain. We must recognise that it is no longer possible to argue that there has been no progress. The many tribes that make up modern Britain are actively making change happen on the ground.

Part II presented a range of statistics to paint a general picture of a changing social and political landscape in Britain. It represents a much more complex country, radically less pervaded by racism than it was fifty years ago. The legal framework was a necessary foundation for those battles against discrimination and Part II

78 T. Hunt, op. cit., p. 14.

aimed to reflect on the successes that are beginning to emerge as a consequence. The rule of law remains our strongest weapon against bigotry, discrimination and structural disadvantage.

Let's assume that the criminal justice system and policing will remain stubbornly disproportionate in their effects on young Black men. The reality is the overwhelming majority of people of colour in Britain do not have life-changing encounters with the police or the criminal justice system.

BAME people are not all forever suffering as victims, and they should not be treated *a priori* as such. One of the persistent truths in policing London has been, how-ever, that a young Black man is still much more likely to be stopped than anyone else. We can guarantee that some of these encounters will be unprofessional, rude and physically abusive. Although disproportionality is falling, it remains stubbornly high. We can fight this without saying the whole system is corrupt.

In dozens of reports for BBC News over two dec-ades looking at inner-city gang culture and related crime, I inevitably saw a large number of young Black boys and girls getting sucked into this street life. This is an uncomfortable truth that needs addressing so that the right remedies can be found. Persistently racialising the problem is not helping us find solutions. There is, for example, abundant evidence to say that young gang members suffering from severe mental-health issues including 'trauma' do not get appropriate care. In which case, because gang members are unwilling to engage with mental-health services in hospital, the institutions capable of delivering such care should focus on delivering that care rather than devoting resources to schemes that focus on their 'racial' identity.

Individual hate crimes including murder, terrorist atrocities and a range of lesser infractions show just how far minds filled with racism can still destabilise communities and weaken cohesion. I am not arguing that racism is a thing of the past. There is no doubt in my mind that the Macpherson Inquiry was a watershed precisely because the racist murder of Stephen Lawrence and the police foul-up in its wake shocked people out of a kind of complacency. This case showed without a doubt that, to some racist White thugs, Black lives didn't matter.

Unfortunately, that robust report, which identified a systemic failing in policing and criminal justice, has left a legacy for many White people that implies that even when a White person is well-meaning they can be racist. This implication has seemingly led to a greater polarisation of discourse rather than a greater meeting of minds in dealing with the unconscious bias and discrimination that persists in Britain.

I have found, for example, this polarisation leads to the difficulty of challenging people when they say that even if they have no issues with Black/White people they would never marry a Black/White person because they wouldn't want to 'water down' their genes. It is not possible to water down your genes. As a person of mixed heritage, I don't make any apologies for objecting to that kind of flawed 'race-thinking', whomsoever the Black/White purveyor of such myths might be.

On the one hand, the cause of diversity is in danger of pushing on beyond the structures that remedy disadvantage, into regulating behaviour in a way which often assumes that in a dispute between Black and White, if you are White you are likely to be an unwitting racist and if you are Black you must be, even if you don't know it, a victim of racism.[79] The outing of racists has almost become a rite of passage experience to prove an organisation's diversity credentials, including within the media. By embracing the mantra of diversity or sympathising very loudly and publicly, there is a belief that we have *ipso facto* moved beyond discrimination simply by being able to share the pain of the victim. I suspect this could account for a number of stories that appear in the media under a 'racism' headline. Often it is simply thuggery, ignorance or rudeness that have triggered the incident in the report.

The uncomfortable truth is that whilst skin colour can still have a bearing on progression and opportunity for individuals, this all-encompassing approach can foster a climate of fear and suspicion in which BAME employees find that managers are unwilling to deal with issues for fear of being drawn into a discussion that pinpoints 'race' as a central issue. Where school managers, police

---

79 This is the premise of Ta-Nehisi Coates's US bestseller *Between the World and Me* (Spiegel and Grau, 2015). Whilst this book has much to commend it, it remains an argument rooted in the American historical experience.

hierarchies or editorial chiefs won't deal with issues for fear of harming personal or institutional reputations. In other words, it fosters a victim culture in which identifying racism as a way of dealing with a particular problem may indeed just exacerbate the problem. It can encourage the proverbial ostrich head in the sand response.

It is of course perfectly reasonable to cite examples of racism in schools, public services and prisons and we should accept that there are enduring mythologies in the representation of different groups in Britain, from gang culture to forced marriages and Islamic allegiances that need to be challenged. But when clumsy headlines assert that since the 2000 Race Relations Amendments Act, Britain has fundamentally failed to address racism because so little has changed, I struggle to find in the landscape shift suggested by the statistics in Part II the overwhelming evidence for such a contention.

Sometimes it seems that for 'professional' anti-racists, success *is* failure precisely because projecting failure defends the deterministic outlook we should be shedding.

The overriding question in my mind is whether the

system allows, endorses or ignores such incidents of racism and if there is a systemic response is it proportionate?

The answer to that question is that it almost certainly depends on where you live, what kind of education you have had, what kind of job you do, whether you have an inclusive friendship circle and ultimately whether you act like you are entitled to exploit the talents you have been endowed with or feel like a victim.

From victims into winners

To say you are a victim of the environment is to say that everyone is against you because of your skin colour or your ethnicity. You are wholly dependent on the environment or the elite that fashions change. You become an object and are cast under the spell of external forces. I felt like this through much of my schooling and used university to liberate myself. This is the kind of determinism that Sidney Hook (1902–89) suggests blights lives:

Sickness, accident or incapacity aside, one feels lessened as a human being if one's actions are always excused or

explained away on the grounds that despite appearances
one is really not responsible for them ... Our dignity as
rational human beings sometimes leads us to protest,
when a zealous friend seeks to extenuate our conduct on
the ground that we were not responsible (we didn't know
or intend what we were doing etc.), that we really are
responsible and that we are prepared to take the consequences of our responsibility. As bad as the priggishness
of the self-righteous is the whine of the self-pitying.[80]

A lot of academic debate has identified racism or the racist system as a malignancy in Britain. In this paradigm,
the only salient variable in understanding the life experiences and life expectations of people of colour is 'race',
be that through personal or institutionalised racism.

Anti-racist politics has for too long relied on deterministic explanations and moral rectitude – the Sisyphean
burden of Blackness – which bestows less empowerment
and not more. For me, one of the problems with the
determinism of the anti-racist critique is that it can be

---

80 Quoted in O. Patterson, op. cit.

used to justify, for example, the shortcomings of people who get into trouble with the law. So it becomes a common-sense understanding that if a Black child does badly at school, gets involved in gang activity, gets sucked into the police and criminal justice system, it is because of a public official who is racist or an institutionally racist system. These are the unhealthy conversations I have reported for years. There is an absence of agency and free will in this argument.

To reiterate, I do not dismiss or deny racism exists, but it is a plea to reimagine its scope and meaning. Yet, because the kind of determinism I am describing has become a new form of rigid orthodoxy, people who challenge the assumption that White racism permeates all Black experiences are accused of being 'race' traitors, Uncle Toms or in denial. A White person with similar views would be a closet racist or in denial. This is surely a disingenuous or immature ruse to shut down discussion.

When I visit secondary schools to talk to aspiring 16+ students of all backgrounds, I always ask them first to aspire to taking responsibility for their journey and how they will conduct themselves.[81] Self-esteem must necessarily be associated with making choices and exercising free will in trying to create a direction for your life. The education system has a responsibility to foster these skills and not burden individuals with a sense of predetermined rejection.

Tell a Black child about racism and not about responsibility and see what happens. Tell a Muslim child that the West hates Islam and nothing about citizenship, accommodation and responsibility and see what happens.

I subscribe to the view that we must have a consciousness of how the social and economic milieu we are born into constrains opportunity. There is abundant evidence that, like all disadvantaged groups, individuals protect their self-esteem by selectively valuing those areas in which their peer group is seen to have accrued advantages and by ignoring or devaluing problematic areas of activity. This is why Black children have been

---

81 Along with several hundred other successful people, I have joined Robert Peston's Speakers4Schools programme to share our experiences with comprehensive school students.

drawn to and excel in sport and the performing arts, myself included.

With such a high focus on BAME failure in our research agenda, you would think that high levels of BAME success in Britain are un-researchable because they are so rare and exceptional. Are we to believe that even those successful BAME individuals in our community who are politicians in local councils, MPs or in the House of Lords, sporting heroes, top managers, doctors, academics, teachers, journalists, businessmen and women, ordinary parents and a myriad of other successful types are all toiling under a Sisyphean burden of Blackness? We should be busy researching and explaining what it is that drives and sustains their success and that of so many ordinary mixed families that thrive in modern Britain.

Put another way, if being a victim of the system explains your troubles and makes you feel better about yourself, then what incentive is there as a young person of colour to strive harder? Thank goodness the results reported in Part II seem to indicate the endeavours and talent of the class of 2014 are quashing this myth.

The more one blames the system for poor performance, the more that poor performance can become a self-fulfilling prophecy. For many years it seemed that low school achievement in British schools for many young Black boys was a badge of honour rather than a burden of shame. If you did succeed, this was a problem, and this was not conducive to high self-esteem. How many young boys of colour like myself nearly succumbed to this urban mythology?

The 2014 GCSE results for Black boys and the university entrants for 2015 from the same cohort are recent BAME educational successes that have come despite racist determinists who assert they are *sufferers* of an inferior genetic composition, liberal determinists who say they are *sufferers* without agency of the social and economic environment and those determinists who see them as *products* of culture and ethnicity and therefore believe any success will be transient.

Curiously enough, I have encountered plenty of people who assume that many of my achievements could be put down to some kind of positive discrimination. I can assure them my LSE education was no walk in the park. If we do not encourage young people to be responsible for some of their problems, how can they be certain they are the reason for their achievements?

It is irresponsible, downright demeaning and racist for reporters across the media, researchers in academia and public commentators to insist on presenting all BAME people in Britain as a single homogenous group of no-hopers, burdened by poverty and a paucity of opportunity and angry and embittered about their 'racial' condition. The point here is that the condition may be a very real one in many walks of British life, but skin colour is less and less the key determining factor.

Where does this all end? Logically, it means accepting that people of colour have no individuality, rights or strength of will, and that legitimises the whole deterministic paradigm, exonerating the oppressor because they too can only do what they are preordained to do in this deterministic worldview. Do not for a moment think I am falling into the trap of blaming the victim for their misfortune – I am suggesting the deterministic nature of the debate helps no one.

No, taking responsibility for me has a different meaning. It means working to achieve merit so you acquire the integrity and power to challenge racism where it rears its head. It means challenging racism, but by engaging in the act of de-racialising.[82] It means asserting your right to be equal so you can be de-racialised. For me this is where hope lies, in the struggle for a de-racialised polity where equality and justice do not affirm, but liberate us from racial categories that will keep us imprisoned in a language that people of colour did not invent.

Civil rights champion Revd Jesse Jackson (b.1941) put it another way when he addressed Middlesex University students: 'You need to abandon your minority complex and adopt a majority complex.'[83] To succeed, you need to have the mentality of a winner and not a victim.

---

82 When I speak on behalf of Speakers4Schools, I want to be recognised by all children as offering an insight into how to be a winner.

83 This was on a December 2013 visit to Britain to talk at Cambridge and Oxford University to address the under-representation of BAME students and to Middlesex to address a university with one of the largest cohorts of BAME students.

What are the prospects of a post-racial future?

In order for a 'post-racial' society to really come about we would need to abandon the lethal combination of science, physiological classification and cultural evaluation that was embedded in the consciousness of Western culture for at least three centuries and is now so deeply embedded in our language that even those who baulk against the concept find it difficult to speak in another tongue.

Where 'race' was concerned, power over centuries became embedded in structures and institutional behaviour, which essentially came to revolve around skin colour and ethnicity. We are only now very slowly dismantling these discriminatory barriers. In Britain, this history of 'race' has made us sometimes lazy, even at times deceitful, by searching for explanation for conflict through the colour prism.

The real issue for us is whether we can move to a place where issues are not instinctively 'racialised' and avoid the pitfalls of therefore ignoring the social problems facing us, which may have other causes and explanations, or indeed where the cultural notions of 'race' are only one causal factor amongst many.

We need to be smarter and more open-minded in order to be able to more clearly diagnose the cause of problems facing people in Britain. We need to identify how gender, class, ethnicity and religion coincide to create a deeper understanding of these problems.

If we look back over the period since the first Race Relations Act, much has been achieved to tackle overt hostility and discrimination. But the paradox is that the mechanisms and institutions put in place to defend these human-rights objectives reinforced the categories that have simply no scientific credibility and remain viable categories only in our own imagination.

Combined with successive census classification, these hard and fast 'racial' categories have cemented crude 'racial' notions in everyday private and public discourse where people will always refer you to 'common sense' if you discuss and challenge the fallacy of 'race' with them.

Perhaps I am instinctively biased on this because I have always been so incensed by the notion of 'half-caste' or 'mixed-race'. For me, these have always been pernicious categories which implicitly legitimise the idea that there are pure 'races'. Complete and utter scientific poppycock, but despite this we persist with the talk of 'races'.

Because the language is so familiar in everyday life and permeates common sense in the interactions between different groups of people, it makes the attempts to de-racialise popular culture and discourse even more difficult. Moving beyond common-sense nonsense to a more refined use of language that doesn't 'racialise' all human interaction requires a shift of imagination.

When I observe the 'creative disruption' and explosion of representations of self on social media, in which stereotypes are both presented and challenged on a daily basis, I see in these alternative narratives the slow undermining of the cultural concept of race, because what is 'normative' is in a constant state of flux in this digital world. We can hope that these cumulative assaults on our imagination may indeed lead to us reimagining the world of 'race' and racism.

The role of politics

I am not a politician, but I do have a sense that to believe in a *politics of modernity* it must reflect on the past but not get trapped in it. For the debate we have been having in this book, this presents us with a paradox.

In order to liberate people of colour from the oppression induced by past racial categories, activists needed to embrace those categories. To change the system from within, using politics and the parliamentary process, the arguments needed to be made that inequality and injustice were rooted in the way in which the categories positively encouraged prejudice and underpinned discrimination based on visible racial differences. In this book, I have made an argument that so-called racial differences were rooted in a set of assumptions established by deeply flawed science.

The civil rights successes in America and, to a large extent taking its lead from there, Britain too, owe everything to this political struggle and the people of vision, courage and resilience who undertook it. My generation was certainly the first beneficiary of it. However, in uniting around the notion of 'Blackness' and the inalienable rights of people cloaked in Fanon's 'black skin', it reinforced the very categories that needed dismantling. As a result, a huge amount of political capital has been invested in notions of 'Blackness'.

Having deconstructed and demolished as fundamentally racist the idea that skin colour is anything more than a distraction and that this logically has not the slightest objective, biological foundation, liberals have clung paradoxically to the idea that 'race' remains an essential means of categorising human experience with the same ontological certainty as biological determinism. It is why the concept of 'race' itself is enshrined in law.

In this worldview, as an existential reference point, you can identify and explain the pattern of an individual's life experience by using their skin colour (or indeed their Islamic faith these days). And anyone who has 'one drop' of 'Blackness' in them is to be judged by this measure.

The argument runs something like this. Although 'race' is biologically irrelevant, it remains important because people believe it to be important and the real consequences of this are played out every day in a racist society such as Britain.

It is difficult territory and, recognising the problems

with the language of 'race', we have experimented with alternative categories such as ethnic minority, BME, BAME, all with varying degrees of success. With most of them we remain uncomfortable and sceptical. In the end it is only a label. My point is, none of these labels identify with any degree of accuracy the qualities of the individual or their life experiences. At the limit, it simply identifies *one* of the numerous barriers to progression in life they might face.

Over time, these categories have in any case changed. As improbable as it sounds, a century ago Irish people were regarded as 'Black' in America. The political struggle of the Irish led first to independence from the English and then in America to a progressive assimilation into White-ness with all the social advantages that brought.

I suppose the fundamental question is what does BAME, BME, Black or ethnic minority actually mean in delivering public policy, public services and opportunity? Are there key experiences these defined groups share in common or is it becoming a less helpful way of thinking about how we eliminate the problems of disadvantage, discrimination and bigotry?

It is not uncommon for people who critique this need to embrace 'Blackness' as a fundamental organising principle in politics, to be accused of being 'Uncle Toms', 'Coconuts', 'Conservatives', 'Self-loathers' or just plain old sell-outs. And yet, in a society with so many mixed relationships and mixed-heritage children, this suggests a potential future replete with self-loathing and denial on a colossal scale. It is a distraction.

As a journalist, when I have investigated gang culture or gun crime or poor attainment at school, it is not so much 'Blackness' that has struck me as the key issue but poverty and inequality. In which case it is not anti-racist measures as such that will navigate a route out of the problem, but anti-poverty measures. By confusing the two and focusing on race, the solution is 'racialised'.

In this jumbled language, logic itself becomes jumbled. My English, Irish and Nigerian genes give me a multitude of ethnicities; I also have German cultural roots and was raised and live in London. But the 'one drop' deterministic world of racial categories overrules all that lived experience because of my skin colour. Now that's the dogma I've been consciously trying to escape from since my innocent remarks in the bicycle seat fifty years ago. Like many people in Britain, I am genuinely a mixture of all of these elements and the whole is more than the sum of its parts.

What I have often asked myself rhetorically is this: what is so special about Whiteness that my African heritage somehow taints it and therefore I must ignore that Whiteness? Since my teenage years, this has always acted as a personal metaphor for the 'racialised' world we inhabit, and it is why I have always chosen to resist the labels of Black or White.

In a sense, the issue here is that the evidence shows that people believe what they want and create distinctions in an arbitrary fashion. Calling someone an ethnic minority or from a 'race' is no more than superficially helpful to identifying human differences. It is something we use to orient our imagination.

In politics, 'race' became a benchmark of what you are 'for' and what you are 'against'. For a hundred years or more it was obvious what this political critique was fighting against: slavery, prejudice, disenfranchisement, oppression, discrimination, disadvantage, injustice and inequality. But now, if it is less obvious what this kind of politics is fighting for and there is more common ground between those formerly known as 'races', politics should change.

Changing the way we talk about race

Although we have become more sophisticated in our census classifications, there is a real danger that these have simply become wedded to outdated modes of differentiation.

We need to change the language of how we talk about each other and if we must use the term 'race' we should use it loosely, *descriptively* but not *prescriptively*. Black and White have become such loaded terms that they divide families, brother and sisters, parents and children. We should abandon them too for the purposes of public policy. It reinforces the myth that there is some biological notion of 'race' to which we should give credence.

We should not ignore evidence of racism, but it shouldn't be the first port of call for all that affects us in life as individuals. We should stop over-racialising our discussions of the problems faced by people of colour. Not all prejudice is racism. Racist language and racists refer to a particular kind of behaviour. But the 'racist' slur is used too easily. There are committed racists and we demean debate when we label people racist when in fact they are simply boorish, thuggish or plain ignorant.

The endless stream of criticism that presupposes that all people of colour suffer as a consequence of their interaction with White people is not only preposterous but is counter-productive and arguably racist itself.[84] It discounts the change on the ground, with hundreds of thousands of mixed relationships and mixed families in Britain today.

Raising the racism complaint can wear thin on those who do not act in a way to harm the interests of people of colour and who actively support change through their own interactions all the way to marriage or parenting. You cannot claim or convince a whole class of people they are something they are not; that has echoes of prejudice.

I have encountered thousands of White people in my

---

84   T-N. Coates, op. cit.

life, including in my own family, who recognise and respect my achievements and yet they have not had an iota of the good fortune that has come my way. It is very difficult to say to them that my skin colour has held me back or that I could have done better if I was White. I could certainly have done things differently if I hadn't been born into a working-class family in north London! I need to retain a sense of perspective as a person of colour even if I accept that my skin colour has worked against me at some points in my life.

Of course racism exists. Call it hatred of 'the other', prejudice, bigotry, xenophobia – there are still a sufficient number of people in Britain who have nothing but ignorance in their heads, contempt in their manners and hate in their hearts for the other. It is they who keep racism alive even in the absence of 'race', but now I believe they no longer operate in the 'soul' of this society but increasingly at its margins.

Inequality and the rising income differentials between the richest and the poorest are structural problems that need to be addressed urgently. But focusing on those in need will not necessarily be helped by identifying the colour differences rather than the educational gaps, the social capital deficits, the poor housing conditions and a raft of other things that stand ahead of skin colour in denying opportunities to millions of young Britons of all colours.

There has been a dramatic demographic shift in Britain and we can't turn the clock backwards to when White people only were in charge. As an optimist with his glass half full, I would say people of all skin colours will have to get used to the idea that BAME Britons will increasingly be in charge of making key decisions (that doesn't mean White people won't be) based not on skin colour but qualifications, talent, experience and confidence.

People will increasingly have to compete on competence and ability and there will inevitably be those who resent this and sink back into the language of racial hatred bequeathed to us through centuries of White supremacy. That may well be a profoundly uncomfortable experience for some people, but the more new BAME graduates that join the job market, the more people will get used to it.

The question I have been addressing here is whether

Britain remains a society with systemic racism that is supported by the state, public and private institutions, or whether Britain is finally beginning to lay the foundations of a level playing field where being BAME is no longer a guarantee of automatic disadvantage and a barrier to advancement.

The battles our forebears fought bequeathed us an opportunity to construct that level playing field using the rule of law. It is not for us to lose sight of this in our disappointments. We must not be diverted or befuddled by a new linguistic mire where we uphold the mythical gods of 'race' as something that can protect us through a kind of racial exclusivity. There is an assumption that progress means that our gains will be permanent. This would be a big mistake. Progress is always reversible.

Let me reiterate to avoid misunderstanding: racism does still exist. But for more and more people it is not the principal prism through which they experience life in Britain. And although we don't live in a 'post-racial' society, we can aspire to it, but only if we dispense with the idea that the fundamental struggle over 'the other' – us and them – is a 'racial' struggle, that racism versus anti-racism is the only dialectic. What happens when the anti-racist becomes racist in their demands for us to accept a new orthodoxy?

Recognising that racism and disadvantage persist should not mask the need to challenge the language of 'race'. By the same token, the transformations in British society should not make us complacent and, to paraphrase President Barack Obama, assume that racists no longer exist simply because people recognise that it is impolite to call someone 'nigger'.[85]

We will never be rid of difference, nor the primordial sense of 'them and us'. In this sense, racism is not irrational. But what will become increasingly clear is that there are other things beyond skin colour which bind or separate us.

Racial determinism cannot deliver justice, equality and fair play for all. This can be achieved only by a

---

85 President Barack Obama, in conversation with journalist Marc Maron in June 2015, said, 'Racism, we are not cured of it. And it's not just a matter of it not being polite to say nigger in public … That's not the measure of whether racism still exists or not. It's not just a matter of overt discrimination. Societies don't, overnight, completely erase everything that happened 200 to 300 years prior.'

coalition of those striving for justice, equality, freedom and fair play. Keeping hope alive means recognising the limitations of 'race logic' and building on the successes of our accidental modern social experiment. Our cosmopolitan future will be built on the gradual acceptance of our cosmopolitan roots.

Under the *rule of law* we can aspire to the goal of inclusivity, where talent is not colour-coded and opportunity to exercise and harness that talent is not thwarted by cultural racism. Where access is open and judgement and progression are based upon principles that can be upheld. I hope this book offers those who believe in this kind of vision of a 'de-racialised' Britain the courage to pursue that goal because they know they are not alone.

I did not choose 'race'; someone chose it for me. It is the key to understanding the melancholy and hope in my argument. I long ago decided I did not want to perform the duties of 'race', but rather struggle to have Kurt Barling judged on his merits. Perhaps that lies at the root of my cosmopolitan sense of fairness: that we be judged, all of us, on our merits. I believe 'race' has run its useful course and the Britain of my children is one where the sheer weight of numbers and talent should gradually turn our minds to the enduring sources of inequality and difference. To paraphrase Revd Jesse Jackson, we can die together as fools or live together as brothers and sisters.

ALSO AVAILABLE FROM BITEBACK PUBLISHING

AUTHENTICITY IS A CON
PETER YORK

REFUSING THE VEIL
YASMIN ALIBHAI-BROWN

THE MADNESS OF
MODERN PARENTING
ZOE WILLIAMS

DOWN WITH THE ROYALS
JOAN SMITH

WHAT HAVE THE IMMIGRANTS
EVER DONE FOR US?
KELVIN MACKENZIE

WHY WOMEN NEED QUOTAS
VICKY PRYCE

HARDBACK, £10

PROVOCATIONS

A groundbreaking series of short polemics composed
by some of the most intriguing voices in contemporary
culture, edited by Yasmin Alibhai-Brown.

— AVAILABLE FROM ALL GOOD BOOKSHOPS —

WWW.BITEBACKPUBLISHING.COM